D0195148

LIVING DELIBERATELY

The Discovery and Development of Avatar®

by Harry Palmer

Cover Design, Book Illustrations & Layout
Nestor L. Sanchez

Editorial Assistance
Kayt Kennedy
Joan Babcock

All our love to all the people that contributed
to the creation of this book.

LIVING DELIBERATELY
© Copyright 1994 by Harry Palmer.
ALL RIGHTS RESERVED

No part of this book may be used or reproduced in any manner what-
soever without written permission from the publisher.

Star's Edge International
237 North Westmonte Drive
Altamonte Springs, Florida 32714

ISBN: 0-9626874-3-X

Avatar® , Creativism™ and Living Deliberately ™
are the registered marks of Star's Edge, Inc.

Publisher's Note and Disclaimer:

LIVING DELIBERATELY is the first section of a larger body of original work collec-
tively referred to as the Avatar Materials. The characters and events described in the text
of LIVING DELIBERATELY are intended to entertain and teach rather than present an
exact factual history of real people or events.

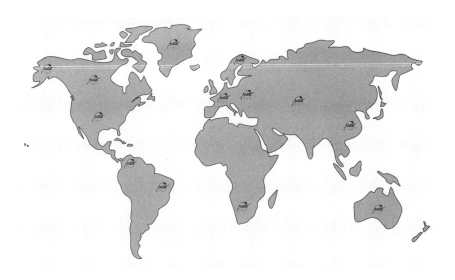

Avatar®

is a seven to nine day self-evolvement course based on principles of consciousness defined and described by Harry Palmer.

Since its introduction in 1987, Avatar has experienced explosive world growth. Today (12/93), there are over 1900 licensed Avatar teachers (Masters) and 25,000 Avatar graduates scattered in 40 countries around the globe. These numbers are expected to double by the end of 1994.

The Avatar Materials are currently available in the following languages:

English	**French**	**Dutch**
German	**Portuguese**	**Spanish**
Italian	**Czechoslovakian**	**Russian**
Korean	**Japanese**	**Chinese**

For the Companions

Table of Contents

Part I

Part II

Part III

Author's Preface

Extraordinary Moments

Have you ever thought about the subject of consciousness? Where would the universe be without consciousness? If you began eliminating things from the universe – suns, planets, spaces, energies – the last thing you would eliminate would be CONSCIOUSNESS!

Could you even eliminate consciousness? Who, or what, would know if you did?

Have you ever been curious, or maybe even concerned, about the momentary experience of some unexpected or unusual mental ability or extra-normal state of consciousness? Maybe you were more than curious; maybe you sought to experience the mysterious state a second time...

Our religious faiths, and more recently our sciences, abound with references to extraordinary consciousness phenomena: enlightenment, turning point experience, holographic consciousness, quantum transformation, cosmic awareness, bliss, nirvana, samadhi, grace, universal harmony, spontaneous healing, alpha rhythms, heavenly rapture, OBE (out of body experience), ESP (extra-sensory perception), levitation, the glory of redemption, the peace of salvation, satori, godhead, Christ consciousness – and this is only a small sampling.

The growing list confirms that more and more people are encountering phenomena that do not fit with their normal waking moments. *Is something going on with consciousness? Is it experiencing its own evolution? A cosmic awakening?*

Extraordinary consciousness phenomena occur spontaneously and do not always fit simple cause-and-effect explanations. People are unsure of how to describe non-physical events. Most of the terminology tends to be esoteric or vaguely fluid in meaning. Comparisons and categorizations are closer to art or analogy than to science. And just when an understanding seems imminent, the event, like a rapidly forgotten dream, fades into a haze of doubt. For a moment there was something unusual...*wasn't there?* Word descriptions are a pale substitute for the real thing.

Instructions or practices that attempt to re-create the phenomena usually condense to some sort of backwards be-do-have ritual that says, "Have faith, do this over and over and maybe something might happen that you could describe as ..." Unfortunately the universe does not work backwards and the only result from such rituals is self-degradation, hypocrisy and pretense.

So people learn to live with the uncertain memory of a few moments, hours or days of an extraordinary experience for which the cause is unknown: a euphoric moment of love, an omnipotent moment of invulnerability, an omniscient moment of crystal clarity, a moment of grace, a moment of premonition, a moment so real that the rest of life seems dreamlike. How can one recover these moments? What combination of thought and event will create them? This is a quest into the quintessential realm of consciousness. The prize is beyond any amount of fame, wealth or power.

Extraordinary moments! Awe-full moments! Experiences that cast even life and death in minor perspective! They leave unexplained magic moments and hint of a thread which, were we able to pull it, might utterly unravel and redefine what we are and what we are becoming.

For some, the demands and desires of life erode such moments into forgetfulness, and they escape back into the safety of plain vanilla reality: paychecks and bills. Probably by now, they will have laid this book aside and continued with the struggle they call their lives.

*But you still read....*For you, a nine-to-five life, while maybe necessary, is not an answer. You're on some sort of quest! Are there some fascinating memories hovering near the edge of your imagination? Would you like to have one more look?

Part I: The Quest

Chapter One

The Sixties

Avatar Master's Course
Orlando, Florida 1993

W inter, 1962. I was walking back from the library one evening when a 1940 green Dodge stopped beside me. It was pulling a silver Airstream house trailer of about the same vintage. It had a spooky feel, as though it had just driven out of a lost episode of the Twilight Zone. I imagined Rod Serling standing up the street somewhere about to do a voice-over: *"For your consideration, Harry Palmer, discouraged engineering student. Like so many of his generation, his mind struggles to understand the path his life is following. In a few moments, his worries will be interrupted as he keeps his appointment with fate...in the Twilight Zone." (music)*

A fogged window rolled down, a gloved hand reached out and presented me with a hand-written invitation. It read:

Awakening: becoming aware that one is conscious

*The Last World Tour of
Swami Ananda!
Experience a last audience with
Swami Ananda before he joins
the Rapture of the Universe!*

*By invitation only,
$5.00.*

Was it coincidence that I was the only person on the street, or that I just happened to have with me my entire life savings of five crumpled one-dollar bills?

* * *

Earlier the same year, I had won a scholarship to Clarkson College of Technology, one of the top engineering colleges in the U.S. – slide rule heaven. Lucky? I don't think so. The scholarship was disaster masquerading as a prize! I would have been better advised to curl up on a tour bus with an encyclopedia. My interest was so broad that details confused me. I was an expert in the entirely superficial, but it was free so I went.

I attended lectures by some of the top mathematical theorists and physicists in the world, but I found only clarified reflections of my own confusions. There didn't seem to be any foundation to what I was taught. I felt as though I had come in on the middle of the show. What a mess. Too late for first principles and too early for conclusions. *This, so this, so this, so this...so what?*

I felt like a bright ape on the bridge of a starship. I learned the punch key combinations for the hatches, but never mind that the starship existed, that someone had a reason for building it, or that it was going somewhere! Immaterial questions. Apparently, no one knew the answers. The patronizing smiles of professors said it was a sign of my immaturity that I even bothered to ask.

So on this night I walked out of the library, beatnik-engineer-poet, folded my *DR. STRANGE* Marvel comic book and headed for the dorm.

* * *

The mysterious green Dodge bounced through the potholes and turned in to Cubbly Park, a small strip of grass and picnic tables along the Raquette River. It stopped in a circle of light under one of the new mercury vapor streetlights and waited. I tried to ignore it. I was on my way to the warmth of the dorm and told myself I couldn't care less about anybody's last world tour. I just wanted...*WHAT!* I turned around and walked back toward the Dodge. *I can't believe I'm doing this!*

"Namasté." A woman's voice – strong Indian accent – greeted me with a word I almost remembered. She appeared from behind the trailer and with a deep bow, identified herself. "I am a disciple of Swami Ananda."

She had a red dot on her forehead and wore a bright orange shawl. At first she looked like a young girl and then like an older woman. I had trouble focusing on her features. *Is she old or young? I can't tell.*

"You may see the Swami immediately," she said and held out her hand for my money. I surprised myself by giving it to her. She folded the dollars and placed them in a small beaded purse. *There goes the Dilly burger #2 with strawberry shake.*

"What is your name, young seeker?" she asked.

"Harry." *How old are you anyway?*

"I must tell you, Mr. Harry, the Swami has not spoken aloud for twenty years, but he knows your every thought and will communicate through me what it is that you most need to learn!" As if to demonstrate the strange arrangement, for a moment she seemed to turn transparent and disappear. I rubbed my unbelieving eyes.

A telepathic holy man! An invisible woman whose age changed every time I looked at her! *What have I gotten myself into this time?*

The disciple opened the door and indicated that I should sit on a red cushion at one end of the trailer's single room. The trailer rocked under my weight as I stepped in. *Candle wax and incense.* As my eyes adjusted to the flickering candle light I saw a beatific old man sitting on a folding chair. *Does he always ride back here?* His eyes were closed and he seemed to be asleep – or maybe dead! I remembered a rumor from school about a mummified corpse in the upstairs closet of the Odd Fellows' hall.

Without my noticing, the woman stepped into the trailer behind me. Floating like some ghost, she settled beside me and bowed to the old man. He didn't move a hair. *Oh, God,* I thought, *Ripley's Believe It Or Not Freak Show! A dead holy man being pulled around in a travel trailer and I paid to see him.*

The woman announced loudly, "Swami Ananda, I wish to introduce you to one who seeks **the great answers.**" *He didn't move.*

For several minutes no one spoke, no one moved. I stared with morbid curiosity at the old man. *Are you dead or alive?* Finally the woman nodded her head in acknowledgment as if something had been spoken. I heard nothing, but I suddenly noticed a sheet of writing paper on the floor in front of me that I hadn't seen before. The woman handed me a pencil and said, "The Swami is honored to meet you at last, Mr. Harry. He wishes for you to draw him a circle."

The statement surprised me. *...honored at last? Has he been expecting me?* Suddenly my arm was covered with goose bumps. It was probably from the cold, I told myself. Anyway, I drew the circle.

The woman approved. "Thank you, Mr. Harry."

Then she placed the paper on a tray and held it before the Swami. *He moved! He is alive!* Without opening his eyes or uttering a word, he picked up the pencil and drew a smaller circle inside my circle and a larger circle outside my circle. Three concentric circles!

For a moment the woman seemed to faint, then revived enough to fold the paper and present it solemnly on upturned palms.

The great answers.

"Thank you," I said. *Who are you? Why do you appear to be every age at once?*

The trailer rocked again as I climbed out. I began to wonder if someone was playing a joke on me. A fraternity prank? That was it, I was sure. I walked away, crossed the street and perched on the back of a bench. It was cold and started to snow. I wished for a collar button on my corduroy Joey Dee sports jacket. *No drunken laughter. No one around.*

After a bit, the Dodge pulled out of Cubbly Park and came back my way. The windows were too fogged to see who drove. The old Dodges used a small fan on the dash to defrost the windshield and this one wasn't working. Whoever was at the wheel was driving by feel.

As the car drew even with my bench, it slowed and words I had never heard nor will ever forget formed a thought in my head. *I am as old as you imagine me to be. May you grow into the universe, Mr. Harry.*

The Dodge disappeared into the night. I sat for a long time and watched the snow begin to fall. It seemed to be erasing my world.

I left college. I left engineering. I left town. Three concentric ripples from my encounter with the Swami? I went home and took up residence in the basement. My mother worried and my father called me a bum. I slept all day and read all night. Occasionally I attended classes at a local college to study philosophy and English literature.

* * *

Summer, 1965. I worked as a fry cook at the Dog 'n Burger for most of the summer. I saved enough to buy a 1953 flathead Mercury. It was a robin's-egg blue V-8 with a white top. The dealer threw in a pair of moon hubcaps which went on the back wheels. Black rims up front. It was cool. I was cool – too cool in shoulder-length hair to flip burgers. I rolled a pack of Luckies in the sleeve of my white T-shirt and hit the road: Greenwich Village, Haight Ashbury, Berkeley. I had no idea where I was going. Going was enough. Me and the blue Mercury drifted over the next rise, around the next bend. I carried the Swami's circles with me, waiting for them to tell me something. When I needed money I painted motel rooms. Some nights I stopped at coffeehouses and read the poems I had written. Beatnik rhymes and bongo drums. Occasionally someone would pass a hat and I'd make a few bucks, but mostly I painted. Motel rooms always needed painting.

Too cool to flip burgers.

I met friends on the road who were also "going"—Smokey, Rebel and Steve. We went from college to college, eating in student cafeterias on borrowed ID's and, when we were lucky, slept in vacant dorm rooms. We visited communes, bagged food for co-ops and generally hung out in the swelling underground culture that characterized the time.

Steve carried a knife in his boot and it made him limp. Cool limp. He had an empty canister of tear-gas from some protest and claimed to be a recruiter for Students for a Democratic Society. Mostly he listened to rock-and-roll while teaching himself to play an electric bass. *There is...a house... in N'Orleans, they call the ri-i-sin' sun.* He played that song in his sleep.

"You are the Truth which you seek!"

Rebel looked like the Zig Zag man on the cigarette rolling papers, so that's what I called him. He was on a mission to get everyone stoned. He could roll a joint with one hand – at least the first one. He turned us on to smoking grass, and we discussed things like how elves turn into tree stumps if you look too closely. We laughed together, had munchie attacks, and forgot what we were talking about. We forgot a lot. Forgetting felt good. *What were we just talking about?*

Smokey. ...Oh, Smokey! A liberated chick. She booed Maxwell housewife commercials and made love to protest the war. *Where did you end up, girl?*

Me? In my mind I was the hippy version of Roy Rogers. I guess my friends felt the identity, because they called me Cowboy. Long-haired space-cowboy! I wonder if Roy ever wore a ponytail?

I was studying Western psychology and Eastern philosophy and finishing college without attending! Professors who called role learned to skip my name. I wasn't there! I was a test-bright book-ape who wore an ominous black arm band and showed up only for their exams. I was tolerated because it was the radical sixties and college deans were politically careful. Columbia University was closed by student riots. Cornell had its buildings occupied by shotgun toting radicals. Like the song said, *"...the time is ripe for revolution."* It was a dangerous time to be intolerant.

So my education was casual and mobile. The paper with the Swami's circles outlasted the transmission on the Mercury. I drove the car like Robert Mitchum in the movie *THUNDER ROAD.* One day I popped the clutch to make the tires squeal .... It ended up as another rusting ghost in a Pennsylvania junkyard. Scrap metal! I took $25 for it and thumbed a ride west.

Smokey wanted me to meet her in Chicago to protest the convention, at least that was what was on the agenda. I would have made it if it hadn't been for the Zig Zag man. He came back from a Timothy Leary lecture preaching the gospel of acid. He had a dozen purple Ozlies. Sandoz. Four-ways. They called them that, because one tablet would turn four ordinary brains into electric mush. Twelve thousand mics of pure LSD-25! Fifty mics would give you a religious experience, a hundred would make you believe you were God....

"...the time is ripe for revolution."

I graduated with the class of '69. Bachelor of Science with majors in English, history, philosophy and educational psychology! A long way from engineering! After graduation we sat in the quad drinking strawberry Ripple and listening to the sounds of colors, watching envious freshmen with flashlight eyes whose questions left after-images in the air. Vibrations everywhere. *Lucy in the sky with diamonds!*

I really hope none of this offends you, but I'd be betraying dead friends if I didn't tell it like it was. For me, this is the way those days were. Assassinations, nuclear threat and Vietnam. It didn't always look like we were going to make it. Tear-gas and insanity. Body counts. A million bullets found warm flesh in the battle between true believers. Morality was bleeding to death, enough blood to float a supertanker, and in the middle of it all, a man walked on the moon. Live TV, scripture from the moon, *"One small step for man, one giant step for mankind."*

The world and I drifted into and out of things that left deep marks on our collective soul. And the three circles? They accompanied me through the perilous worlds of gradschool, cults and shaman psychedelics. They came to mind when the lyrics of a Bob Dylan song reminded me: *"Naathing is revealed!"* They were there when I swayed with a new bride to

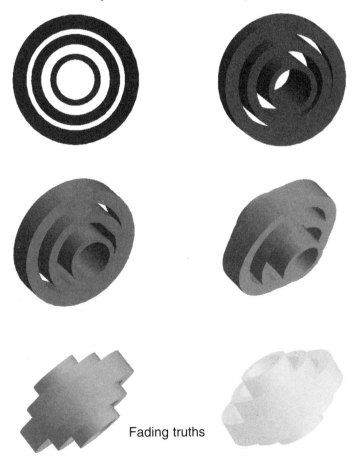

Fading truths

"We're Sgt. Pepper's Lonely Hearts Club Band, we hope that you'll enjoy the show." And they were there a few years later when we wiped tears and said good-by.

Then, like most things, they were lost. As if the truth could ever be lost! Maybe they were left behind as a place marker in one of the books I was reading at the time: *ATLAS SHRUGGED, STRANGER IN A STRANGE LAND, JOURNEY TO THE EAST, SIDDARTHA, THE HARRAD EXPERIMENT, ELECTRIC KOOL-AID ACID TEST, DUNE, THE I-CHING...* I don't know.

Then it was over! Just like that. End of line. Last train to the coast. It was time to get straight.

I cut my long hair and bought a used Robert Hall suit. I moved to the other side of the desk and gave lectures on American literary figures. I shed the sixties like an empty exoskeleton of a cicada clinging to the bark of an oak tree. Bell-bottoms, love beads and dope, Morrison, Joplin and Hendrix, left behind.

The sixties were a decade out of sequence, a serendipitous spiritual experience, wandering possibilities looking for a home. At least, that's how I remember them.

Farewell to the sixties

And somewhere among the possibilities, the circles within circles, the seeds of the Avatar materials began growing in my consciousness.

Chapter Two

Incubation

One day in the early seventies in Los Angeles, I had an extraordinary experience that I would not understand or reexperience until more than a decade later.

I walked out of my apartment and I noticed that my normal perspective had been replaced with a much broader one – a total perspective! My thoughts and the things I looked at were in the same place!

I was walking through a physical landscape that was the same as my mind. Separate from both. What had been inside my mind was now outside! Or maybe the outside was inside? Concentric circles! Something major had dissolved, something that kept the objective and the subjective apart. The world and the mind were suddenly synonymous. A perfect, coincidental alignment of mental thought and physical reality. So simple, so pure! **The mind had become the universe, or perhaps it was the other way around.** I closed my eyes and I could still see! My physical vision and my mental vision were in perfect alignment.

I was astonished at my own calmness. There was an amused relief, like when in the midst of worry one discovers there is no need for concern. The feeling grew until it engulfed everything. It seemed to me to be the quintessential experience of the meaning of the word "okay." Everything was okay. **Everything** was okay! *Had this ever happened to anyone before?*

Who could I ask? *Have you ever felt like I feel? How do I feel? Detached...but okay. Yes! Okay!* I looked up and down the street half expecting the old green Dodge to appear. Nothing!

Later I met a friend, but I was reluctant to talk to her about the experience. I suspected she would frame it in psychological terms and that would mean a discussion which I preferred not to have right then. *Besides, if you discover you've suddenly gone over the edge, there is no sense in broadcasting it!* I just blended into the ranks of those who were pretending to be normal and guided my body to class. Eyes closed!

The body worked fine and went where I sent it, but **on another level** I had the peculiar sensation of being completely behind time and space, not moving at all! Watching, seeing, everything was okay.

* * *

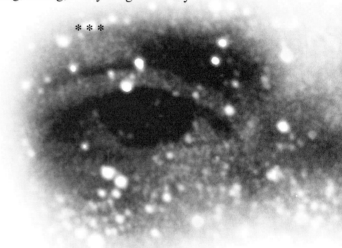

Summer, 1972. I was participating in a spiritual counseling practice* that insisted I go back in time (75 million years, to be exact) and explore my past lifetime memories of a horrible event that was supposed to have destroyed galactic civilization and left worlds in ruin. *Truth or science fiction? The fall of man? Who knows?*

Anyway, I guess I was supposed to cry or emote or something so I could free myself of the terrible trauma that had scarred my consciousness. I was informed that one lady who had already gone through this counsel-

---

* *Scientology*

ing had struggled with the trauma for three days, but then had spontaneously cured herself of cancer and recovered perfect 20-20 vision. So I was excited and ready.

After a briefing on what my donations bought, I was given a thin pack of materials to read about the event. Interesting reading, but nothing much happened. Well, to be honest, nothing happened! I figured I must have had a huge emotional shut-off, subconsciously protecting myself from the horror! Repressed trauma! I knew that was the worst thing. So I started cranking up my imagination to create the most awesome fearful experi-

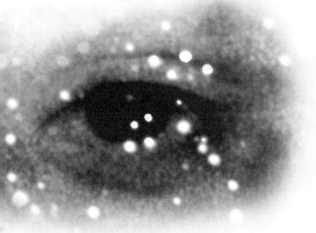

ence that a being or entity could possibly endure. Gravitational fields collapsing. Nuclear incineration. Betrayal. Torture. I shook. I broke out in a cold sweat. I wept. I moaned and writhed on the floor – at least part of me did. Another part of me, the detached part, observed with interest.

Right in the middle of what must have been the most grievous episode of suffering ever to afflict a being, the detached part of me began to wonder: *What if I don't create the memory of this event? I mean, it is **my** mind, right? What if I just stop creating this memory?*

No problem. Seemed like good advice to me. I got up and dusted myself off.

Why was I creating the memory if all I wanted to do was get rid of it? *I think about it so I can stop thinking about it! I wasn't thinking about it in*

the first place! Who is in charge, me or my mind? Does my mind know
something I don't know?

When I volunteered my little insight, I was told very sternly by an Ethics Officer (spiritual practices in those days were very serious) that I was avoiding the incident and that I needed to go back and think about it some more so I could stop avoiding it. I meekly obliged and went back to my room. But my enthusiasm to suffer had suffered. The event taught me two important lessons: one, only a decision is required to change one's mind; and two, I learned not to seek approval for my realizations.**

* * *

I left Los Angeles skeptical of all psychological paradigms that have us bearing the burden of our past around with us – presumably tucked into the wrinkles of the brain or stored electrochemically in some fusion of mind and brain. How much does the past really influence me? I kept asking myself the question: if that made me do this, what made me do that? The detached part of me, which I discovered I could contact by honestly feeling "everything is okay," was amused by the idea that anything could make me do anything – can God create a stone that is so heavy that even he can't lift it? *Maybe, I thought, if He wants to.*

So a piece of the Avatar materials slid into place: the past influences you as long as you let it. From the detached part that was watching, it was perfectly clear, **the past and future do not exist unless I deliberately (or by some default setting) decide to create a memory or image of them in present time. The PAST is not the source of the present; the PRESENT is the source of the past and the source of the future!**

** *In fairness to Scientology's L. Ron Hubbard and his galactic tragedy, it should be pointed out that early Greek philosophers believed that a period of intense contemplation or the witness of tragedy enacted upon a stage accomplished a beneficial purging of a person's own emotional burdens. Homeopathy, as well, believes that 'like cures like' and that having a good cry can have a therapeutic benefit. Perhaps Hubbard's intent was not so much, as his followers believe, to be the literal historian of an event, but was to engage in some homeo-psyche-therapy.*

It's all here, right now! The present is the beginning of time.

Something rejuvenating happened to me when I stopped creating the past. The quest to explore life firsthand resurfaced. Within me there was a hunger for experiential first principles. The real quest! I didn't want so much to know as I wanted to experience! It seemed as if I had been studying someone else's descriptions of life, never mind that I was alive, that my own consciousness was the perfect laboratory in which to find the answer. With that recognition, I became my own friend and began to explore firsthand my own capacity to determine and experience.

The indoctrinations of how one should feel and how one should operate began to fall away. A true sense of personal responsibility awakened. After ten years of spiritual study, I realized that all of what I had learned was what someone else believed – my mind was full of what someone else had concluded or imagined. Thought dragons, keeping me from my own divine center.

I began to gather the courage to do my own imagining, my own believing. I retraced old steps and started over. I discarded any ideas that I had assumed for approval from others. I followed an intuitive feeling that told me that the more information I collected, the further I moved from experiencing. The more reasons why something was true, the less experientially real it became. It was liberating to realize that I didn't know! No pretending. No proselytizing. No more act. I didn't know! But I was alive!

I started feeling, deciding, doing. My philosophy and my experience of life began to converge.

* * *

Seasons,1982. I gave my books away, hundreds of them, and moved back to the land: one hundred and sixty acres on the southern slope of Buck Mountain, New York. An old stone wall (no one could remember who built it) ran around the property. I raised my own food, learned carpentry and back-to-land skills, bartered, and read *Organic Gardening* and *The Mother Earth News*. I waded through three feet of snow to gather firewood. When the spring thaw finally came, the mud was so thick that it sucked your boots

Angel Starbeam Dreamer

Angel Star Dancer

off. I helped a registered Jersey named Angel Starbeam Dreamer give birth to a calf at 4:00 in the morning and then with the sun rising behind them, I watched mother and her wobbly-legged daughter – *Angel Star Dancer* – go to the pond for a drink, What a picture!

The family grew. Pigs. Chickens. Peacocks. Ducks. Geese. And two German shepherds. The farm taught me that there was a difference between being alive, really alive, and just living.

Now the young disciples came to me. They were sure I knew, because I said I didn't know. They didn't know either, but what I accepted matter-of-factly, they resisted. "Tell us what to believe, Harry." *Have any words more dangerous ever been spoken?*

But as long as they helped with the chores they were welcome. When they thought too much I instructed them to seek stillness: "Close your eyes. Look for something in your mind that is not a thought. Concentrate on the space between thoughts." Eventually their mental skies cleared.

The lessons were simple: don't internalize, become absorbed in what you are doing. Chop wood, carry water. It was country Zen. Zen celebrated the fact that you didn't know. The mind was disengaged, which of course, left the experience of life. Chop more wood. Carry more water. Don't let the heart wander. . . .Do you know how boring Zen can get?

I switched my mind back on and began exploring it. Maybe it could find something useful to do since the pond was filling nicely with water and I had enough firewood piled and drying to see me through the next ice age.

I started counseling people with problems and learned to observe and listen closely. Mental patterns began to appear. Little by little I developed a technique. It was like the string that the Purina company sewed along the top of its feed bags. Pull just right and the string unraveled, but pull wrong and it knotted so badly you had to cut the bag open.

When the technique worked, it unraveled and opened to a profound concept: **I create my experiences according to what I believe.** What a peculiar notion! Until now it seemed everyone had assumed that people created their beliefs according to what they had experienced. *What if it was the other way around?*

Here's how it might work. Imagine a universal plasma of total possibility formed and filtered by your beliefs, each belief acting like a tuned filter in a radio receiver, passing only a certain frequency of circumstance and event. And like a radio tuner the belief tends to filter out anything above or below its frequency window. What you believe sets you up to focus on the elements that move from all possibility into the foreground of your experience.

For example, if you believe that walking in the park at night is dangerous, you tend to

Try this little filtering exercise. Say to yourself, "I'm very sad." Imagine it if you have to. Think over the events of the last year and see what your attention focuses on. Take a walk and look around. Notice what stands out.

Now say to yourself, "I'm happy." Again, imagine it if you have to. Think over the events of the last year and see what your attention focuses on. Take another walk and look around. Notice what stands out.

interpret your perceptions according to that belief. Rustling leaves become the footsteps of a mugger. Shadows conceal unimaginable dangers. Your heart speeds up and you experience the park as a dangerous place. Your expectation of harm may even be strong enough to motivate someone who is suggestible into harming you!

Have you ever heard someone say, "I don't know why I did it?" What if they did it because your belief created circumstances which caused their actions? Is it possible? Have you ever acted spontaneously in accord with someone else's expectations? *Try offering your hand to someone to shake.*

Once the filtering belief is installed in your consciousness, **your experience gives you evidence to support what you believe**. A self-fulfilling prophesy. This explains how two people with conflicting beliefs both experience evidence that supports the rightness of their own beliefs and the wrongness of the other's beliefs.

* * *

When the technique appeared not to work, it knotted up like the string at the top of the feed bag. How about chance events and acts of God? What about victims? What if what I experienced had no relationship to what I believed!

Was it possible that I created an experience by believing in it and then forgetting that I had believed it? Yes, I supposed. Did I always know what I believed? Maybe not. I knew what I said I believed, but was it what I really believed? Was what I really believed the motivation for what I said I believed?

Before I went too far, I knew I had to figure out exactly what I believed and what effect it had on my own experience. How does one believe? Where does it start? What are the mechanics of belief? How long do beliefs last? Does it matter what I believe or when I believed it? Were my experiences shaped by **what** I believed about beliefs and/or **how** I believed them?

I played with an interesting bit of logic about personal responsibility: **I experience what I believe, unless I believe I won't, in which case I don't! Which means I did!**

Chapter Three

Tanking

One day my wife Avra came home and found I had replaced the cherry table in her dining room with a 1500 pound sensory deprivation tank.

"Where's the...What's that, a coffin?" The tone of her voice caused the German shepherds to fold back their ears.

"Sensory deprivation tank!" I said proudly. I showed her the hatch and began to explain. I had read about sensory deprivation tanks and thought, *what a great tool for exploring beliefs!*

The tank was a hardened polystyrene foam chamber about eight feet long and four feet square. It contained a solution of water with 800 pounds of Epsom salts dissolved in it. "The water is so saturated with salt that your body floats effortlessly. You lose any sense of gravity. The temperature is brought up to the same temperature as your skin, around 94 degrees, so there is no sense of hot or cold. It is neutral. The tank is so dark that you can't tell if your eyes are open or closed. The tank is also soundproof.

"When you are in the tank, you float weightlessly; there is no sense of feel, no sense of sound, no perception. You are just there, in consciousness, deprived of external sensation and present time experience."

"You're going to get in there?" she asked.

"Yeah." I smiled cheerfully.

"And close the door?" She and both German shepherds peered through the hatch at the swirling water that was trying to dissolve a small mountain of Epsom salt.

"Yeah. As soon as it's ready."

"For how long?" She asked looking wistfully at her dismantled dining room table in the corner.

"Dunno yet." Then I thought to add, "probably not too long."

She shook her head the same way she had when I brought home the first milk cow. "O-o-kay, Harry. I hope you don't drown." *Not in my dining room.*

* * *

For the next eight weeks, I spent most of my time in the tank. The only evidence of my existence was the dried Epsom salt trails leading to the refrigerator and the bathroom. *Happy trails.*

One of the first things that becomes evident during sensory deprivation is that the mind is more than willing to compensate for any lack of sensory input. Sensory input actually keeps the mind somewhat in focus and under control, like wet-sheet wrapping someone who is severely disturbed.

When the body's sensory input is deprived, the mind compensates and becomes a three-ring circus with steam calliopes, high school marching bands and auctioning contests. It is a chaotic experience that somehow you must rise through to reach the stillness beyond mind.

* * *

I float somewhere in the middle of the confusion, quite sure that whatever I am doing is wrong.

Here's what it's like:

How do I tell if I'm awake or dreaming? What's real and what's imagination? Should I meditate on something or just let it happen? What am I supposed to do? Maybe I should read some books on tanking first. No, I can't do that because I am already in the tank. Or am I in the tank? Where am I? Who am I? Am I inside or outside the body? What body? Let's find a place to start. Start what? Who's us? I don't feel anything.

Calm down, I tell myself! But who said that to me? Are there two of me? How many selves do I have? One sounds like my dad. What's going on? Why am I talking to myself? Why did I ask that? Who did I ask it of? I'm still talking to myself. Don't I know what I know without asking or saying it to myself? There, I just asked myself that.

This is incredible! It's like my own private Thoughtstorming* session! But I'm the only one here. Who did I say that to?

Instant insanity! Man goes insane in tank.

Am I still in the tank?

I forgot.

Yes, I'm floating in a tank. But where?

I'm not floating in a tank; I'm floating in a mind. Why did I say that to myself? Why didn't I just know that?

Why did I ask that? What's going on here? How could I not know? I give up.

Okay, anybody gets to say anything he wants.

---

*Thoughtstorm is a registered trademark of Star's Edge, Inc. It refers to a technique used to create synergetic thinking in a group.

Anything?

No resistance.

Until we come up with an answer that everyone agrees on.

What's the question?

Who am we?

Days later, the subtle perceptions that exist beyond the thinking-mind began to turn on. It was like a room with a rock-and-roll band playing full throttle, and in a corner was a portable radio playing classical music with the volume set very low. You had no idea the classical music even existed until the band took a break. That's what happened. The Mental

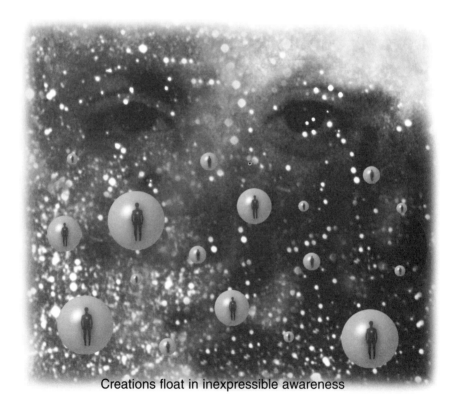

Creations float in inexpressible awareness

Rhythm Band grew exhausted and took a break!

I began to wake up as who I was. Not know, but experience. What a surprise! It was that old detached higher self part of me that watches interestedly without judging. *"How you been?"* I asked myself. As always the answer was, *"Okay."* After integrating this new viewpoint, I began exploring the subtle background images that surround the thinking-mind: resisted experiences, conceptions, births, traumas, deaths. The entire record of the existence of who I thought I was floated like a bubble in a sea of inexpressible awareness. At another level of being **I was** the sea of inexpressible awareness.

I watched the illusion of substance and separation unfold. Lifetimes after lifetimes. Lives within lives. Parallel lives sharing lessons. And the inexpressible awareness, the-always-present, watched silently from its spacelessness.

Creations floated like bubbles, each containing and defining a separate measure of awareness – seminal selves! Bubbles collapsed and merged into one another until they disappeared or until they reached that remarkable threshold quantity of consciousness that blurted forth, **"I am."**

Here was where the lessons of Avatar unfolded, watching consciousness define itself from the void, rising and ebbing in that no-space sea of inexpressible awareness.
From this viewpoint a thought form can be

Awareness plus limit equals consciousness. Awareness without limit is inexpressible. Even to describe it as inexpressible is to define something less than awareness without limit!

perceived or apperceived (meaning perceived without the use of sensory organs.) **It is something!**

This was another revolutionary idea! Do you know how long people have been studying consciousness with the assumption that it was made of nothing rather than that it was made **from** nothing? Something from nothing – primal creation.

* * *

There are several levels in the cycle of conscious activity – different concentrations of definition and awareness. For example, I can create a mental image of a tree – that is one level of conscious activity. I can create doing something with that mental image – that decision is another level of conscious activity. I can then carry out my decision to modify the image of the tree and monitor or correct what I decided to do. That is still another level of conscious activity.

As the point of view changes, the character of what is apperceived changes. From one level of consciousness the subject of time appears thus: I am in the present moment. There is a past, and there is a future.

Moving to another level there is only the present moment, and in this present moment I create an idea called *"past,"* an idea called *"present time"* and an idea called *"future."* Rather than being an instant in time between a *"past"* and a *"future," "now"* becomes timeless NOW containing these ideas about time. From this level the past doesn't exist or influence me unless I choose, or feel the need, to create it!

Move up another level and the concept of time disappears all together. All that is, was, or ever will be blends into a singular, motionless trace upon infinite awareness. Time becomes the sequence in which things are contemplated. From here, unified life can contemplate the whole space-time fabric of existence simply as self: **all possibilities occurring simultaneously.**

* * *

I had a realization. Truth is relative to the point of view from which it is perceived. What I look **as** and where I look **from** determine my perception of truth.

I experienced deep compassion as I understood that everyone, from their viewpoint, is seeing truth. I think this is a key understanding for creating a harmonious civilization.

Instead of asking if something is true or not, I could ask: **"From what point of view or from what definition of consciousness is the statement true? From what point of view or from what definition of consciousness is the statement false?"**

Realitivity is the ultimate truth! Had Albert Einstein had a tank, he might have understood this sooner.

Avatar Masters Course
Orlando, Florida, 1992

AWARE: Watchful; vigilant; knowing
WILL: The power to decide; to direct; to decree
Feel what it feels like to be only...effortlessly... AWARE WILL.

Cures for Going Mental: For any question beginning with "why" the answer is "because"; for any question beginning with "can" the answer is "yes."

Chapter Four

I Am Still Floating

Still floating, I asked my bubble-selves:

Are stones and ideas different concentrations and different frequencies of the same stuff? What stuff? What are the choices? Knowing and not-knowing. Consciousness? Inexpressible awareness shaped by definition into fields of familiarity. Is reality really familiarity? Is the process of examining really one of creating?

Take the definition away from stuff and what do you have? Universal plasma? Definitionless stuff. Stuff without edges. Non-dimensional, timeless awareness without object or content. The world and consciousness are made from the same awareness that underlies both!

Assumptions prepare the stage. And the total of all the assumptions...what about the rock? Is it just a very solid assumption? Is it possible that "rock" and "idea of rock" are merely describing different concentrations of assumption? Strata of rock. Densities. Precipitation of assumption. The universe precipitating under the deliberate intention of the aware will.

And what about the mind? Consciousness? Packets of awareness separated by self-definition.

The mind permits us to focus on the physical universe. At one stratum (in one bubble) all the assumptions equal the mind, but in the next stratum up (the next bubble out), all the minds are assumptions! Assumptions that think.

Concentric circles! Namasté, Swami. I begin to understand.

Assumptions nestle inside assumptions like cups inside cups. Little bubbles inside larger bubbles. Atoms in molecules. Molecules in compounds, and so on...definitions in a unified field of inexpressible stuff... **which is aware.**

As long as no one asks me to explain anything, I know it all. I am tiptoeing out of the theater where the universe is playing!

Little lifetime theaters within theaters. Playing thought excerpts from the life and times of me. No need to dress for the theater. I write the script. I am the star. I am the villain. I am the stage.

At some level I secretly play the audience as well. Life is truly an extraordinary event!

Did I come created with a mind? What do I do? I desire. I resist. Is the mind just recordings and distortions of what I have desired and resisted? Assumptions that define and preserve experience? Assumptions put on automatic. Default assumptions. Where do the thoughts come from?

Occasionally a drop of condensation fell from the ceiling of the tank and made a horrendously loud, slow-motion ...ker-plunk!

Desires. Resistances. They are the motives that direct life when I don't. They invite the creation of assumptions. This is good. This is bad. Assumptions become beliefs! Thoughts arise from beliefs! Beliefs are seed pods of thoughts. Beliefs ripen and when disturbed, shed thoughts, defining them in bubbles of consciousness to drift upon awareness until they dissolve.

...Ker-plunk!

I am a belief that believes! I am...A CREATION WITHIN THE CREATOR, A CREATOR WITHIN THE CREATION. I am a bridge between awareness and creation. The middle circle! The one the Swami had me draw! I package awareness in definition and then wear it like a suit of clothes. Awareness in perfect conservation, settling back into its inexpressible self. Rhythm. Breath. Life. The mind thinks, the background decides! Move to the background, live deliberately.

Something fell out of nowhere. A spinning, glistening, crystalline drop of near-truth. It was simple; it was profound. Life is a dance of consciousness.

...Ker-plunk!

I AM! The birth cry of consciousness. Awareness defined. I AM. Existing at the core of self. Existing at the beginning of space. I AM NOT. The death of consciousness. Awareness released from definition. I AM NOT. Existing beyond the edge of defined self. Life and death, a simple stirring within the source of all.

I am is a bridge between awareness and creation.

Chapter Five

Notes From The Tank

During the period I was floating, I kept an old typewriter on the top of the tank and from time to time would lift myself up through the hatch of the tank and tap out some "near-truth" that I didn't want to forget.

There is a difference between knowing
intellectually and experiencing. The
intellect is a product of consciousness
and cannot know beyond the limits that
consciousness assumes. To go beyond the
limits of the intellect one must experience firsthand without evaluation.
Intellectual understanding is a finished
jigsaw puzzle, picturing some experience
in words.

Experience is being present, without definition, expectation or judgment, with
one's perceptions.

* * *

The cycle of genesis is imagination,
intention, creation, perception, experience...over and over. All of which is
occurring against an aware, compassionate
no-space background-the detached higher

self, pure awareness!

***

There are methods by which one can fluid-
ly move from one definition of consciousness to another. One can change!

The level of idea you look AS determines
the level of idea you look AT.

If you want, you can break anything down
to increasingly finer parts while at the
same time shrinking with your perception.
Or you can expand yourself and start
looking at increasingly larger things.
Zero and infinity. The alpha and omega.
The inner and outer circles.

***

Awareness defines itself to create consciousness. Getting into and analyzing
the content of consciousness is the
process known as trying to figure it out.
It always comes down to saying that that
bubble means this when looked at from
this bubble. Relativity.

Awareness waits in the background, totally compassionate, appreciatively watching.

***

Attention makes a creation more solid and draws it into one's life.

Judgments placed on a creation cause it to be either desired or resisted.

Either resisting or desiring results in the attraction of the creation that is the subject of one's attention.

Gravity and attention are probably different modalities of the same force.

The ability to relocate consciousness is the ultimate form of space travel.

* * *

It is possible to return to the source of a creation. Once there, it is possible to stop creating a creation by relaxing into an effortless state (discreate).

* * *

The difference between awareness and consciousness is that consciousness has content, extension in time and space, and form. Consciousness is a less solid material universe. And similar to the growth and decay of the material universe – but by a different pattern – consciousness is subject to expansion and contraction according to its alignment with cosmic forces. The ancient Tao!

Between the normal waking consciousness
and the inexpressible background of definitionless awareness are the confining
rings of desired and resisted creations.
With the proper tools, a being can learn
to navigate these rings and arrive at the
totally-knowing compassionate background
from which the final and total content
and form of consciousness is apperceived.
This is enlightenment.

* * *

All the ideas we have of ourselves are
ULTIMATELY false. Any asserted or resisted definition – call it I, identity, self
– it is not who we are! It's a product of
who we are! It's the bubble we created
to operate from within. It is the definition that we wear, and it determines our
experience of other bubbles. Ego is the
effort to protect the bubble.

A self is an idea that awareness is tem-
porarily availing itself of for the purpose of experiencing certain other ideas.
The self is a means of participating in a
paradigm. It is possible to change self
or even to go beyond self altogether.

* * *

From the Vedas: "What is within us is also without. What is
without us is also within. He who sees difference between
what is within and what is without goes evermore from death

to death." From Avatar: "Move into the background, live deliberately"

* * *

Palmer's Scale

   Inexpressible Source
   Awareness (Light)
   Definition (Creation/Discreation)
   Consciousness
   Existence (Now)
   Space (Viewpoint)
   Observation
   Attention
   Time (Duration)
   Judging (Labeling)
   Emotion (Response)
   Thinking (Resistance)
   Disregard (Ignore)
   Identity
   Forgetfulness (Unknowns)
   Random Circumstance
   Elements (Matter)
   Decay (Collapse)
   Alternate Realities
   Inexpressible Source
   Etcetera

* * *

The size of the bubble is determined by the responsibility you assume, and this size determines whether something is within you or outside you. Definitions eventually integrate. If you assume a

The miracle is not that there is life within the universe; the miracle is that there is a universe within life.

Truth is camouflaged by its simplicity.

very small, infinitely small, level of being then everything appears to be outside you. That's maximum separation from awareness. You have become a physical particle!

On the other hand, if you assume a level of being that is expansive enough to contain the universe, then the universe is within you.

* * *

In a rush of light, I pushed open the lid of the tank for the last time. My skin looked like prunes. The quest was successfully concluded. Last question. End of the line. The great answer! The brush-strokes upon the unknown were mine!

I rocked the tank as I stepped out. The condensation on the ceiling of the tank fell in a shower of droplets. Hundreds of ker-plunks! Each sent three ripples across the surface where I had been floating. Ripples that inter-mingled in a holographic reflection of the world. It was a message.

Yes, Swami, I am indebted. Before I join you, in your ageless forms, I will mark the trail for others.

Avatar Master Course
France, La Grande Motte, 1991

Chapter Six

The Rapture

What lies between us?
Only our creations!

September, 1986. I drained and dismantled the sensory-deprivation tank. In many ways it was a useful tool, but I now realized it was unnecessary to spend any further time in the tank. I saw clearly that there were easier ways to achieve the long-sought, high ground of awareness from which any existence is a profound experience. If someone had said to me, *you're out of your mind,* I could have replied, *that's true.*

I now saw the mind as a universal tool that could be adjusted, aligned and changed. It was no longer a prison or a trap. I was, delightedly, awake in the void!

How did I feel? As I decided to.

I could determine, as easily as I could shift attention from one sound to another or from one sight to another, the form and content of the consciousness I defined myself as. I could experience any state of existence I could imagine, any state I wished to create. So, naturally, I chose to be euphoric. And when I created it, the whole universe reflected my expectations back to me. I choreo-

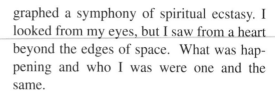

When you adopt the viewpoint that there is nothing that exists that is not part of you, that there is no one who exists who is not part of you, that any judgment you make is self-judgment, that any criticism you level is self-criticism, you will wisely extend to yourself an unconditional love that will be the light of your world.
—Harry Palmer

graphed a symphony of spiritual ecstasy. I looked from my eyes, but I saw from a heart beyond the edges of space. What was happening and who I was were one and the same.

I retreated to Buck Mountain to explore this new existence and to enjoy a glorious fall. I had the prize so long sought, the elusive extraordinary moment of consciousness deliberately created. I was in whatever place and time I created. In full view was the ever-changing expression of the universal consciousness. I saw the end of the path that every spiritual practice, in its purest moment of conception, has attempted to bring to humankind. I saw the possibilities and the pitfalls, the halls of mirrors that words can become. I saw how righteous folly could turn even the noblest path into the wheel ruts worn by "civilized" armies.

I knew the simplest of truths. I was because I said I was. I knew the truth was not what I or anyone else created, but the truth was that we created it. I understood that the consciousness in all living things was individualized only by **what** they created, not by the fact **that** they created. Beneath the definition, beneath the illusion of difference, I felt a universal self, and though it still slumbered, it was unified and whole. Beyond the dream theaters of consciousness, beyond the creations of time, form and event, I experienced a total compassion and unconditional love for life. I could stay or return. The choice of the bodhisattva!

I was not in the world nor of the world, but within **what was possible** a small bubble floated. It contained the universe.

I watched the mountain ash leaves dance brightly and blow orange and yellow in the wind. Galaxies floated in the universe. A shimmering veil of creation. An ancient orchestration of belief. There was unity, and within that unity there was a watching and a spiraling of orange and yellow leaves. There was no separation between the watching and the spiraling.

And I smiled a lot. He, who lived in the bubble, smiled a lot...

Chapter Seven

The First Avatars

November, 1986. There were nine people in the first test group. They included my wife and her staff at the Creative Learning Center. Most of them had delivered and received many hours of regressive type psychotherapy – reliving traumas, releasing pain, resurfacing emotion, etc.

The majority of their clients were appreciative and had experienced a lessening of life's tensions. So they were understandably skeptical about my new Avatar processes.

"Where did you get that name, Harry?"

"It's been around," I replied.

"Aren't you afraid it's going to offend people?"

"I don't think so," I said. *Only the special ones,* I thought.

We had coffee together and I briefed them about my work. I discovered that they were already thinking in terms of "belief precedes experience." There was some resistance, but also they were aware that something transforming had happened to me. I noticed it in their reactions. My presence had a euphoric effect on them that I was not intentionally attempting to create. There was a relaxing of fixed opinions that gradually turned into genuine curiosity.

"Okay, Harry, if your process makes me feel as good as you look, I'm ready."

My wife volunteered to go first. We went upstairs to her office, and I explained that before we started the processes I wanted her to do some preliminary exercises. I asked her to put imaginary labels on things.

"Label that," I said, pointing to a doorknob.

"Doorknob," she played along.

"Label that."

"Telephone."

"Label that."

"Wall."

I noticed that for the most part she was allowing the items I pointed out to suggest their own labels. The typewriter was labeled "typewriter." The desk was labeled "desk."

I kept going. In a few minutes she realized that she was recognizing things rather than labeling them.

"Is there a difference?" she wanted to know.

"What do you think?" I answered in my finest counselor identity.

"Yes, there is. Labeling seems more –I don't know."

"Source?"

"Yes, that's it. Source!"

Now she labeled the telephone "potato," the bookcase "item 67" and a vase of flowers "creation number 5." She remarked that the objects were now more objects than they were words. The room brightened up.

When she was comfortable with that step, I continued with another preliminary exercise, asking her to feel the separation between herself and the things she was labeling.

"Label that."

"Chair."

"Good, can you feel the separation between you and the chair?"

"I'm me and it's it." I observed her settle in and begin to enjoy the game.

"Label that."

"Book."

"Good, can you feel the separation between you and the book?"

"Uh-huh!"

And then I expanded the procedure, still on that first step. "Do you have any ideas about yourself that you don't like?"

"Well, I suppose, sort of." She squirmed, preparing for the invasion of privacy that usually followed such questions.

"Don't tell me about it," I said, "just pick one out and think about it."

She thought for a moment, then said, "Okay, I've got one."

"Label it from source."

"Okay."

"Good, can you feel the separation between you and the idea?"

She muttered a surprised, "Hum-m. I'm me and it's it! That's true isn't it?"

We did a few more ideas, including her own name as a label.

"How do you feel?"

"Aware. That's it. I don't feel like I have to do anything."

I continued with the process and asked her, "Do you have a sense of time?"

"Sure. It's ticking away."

"Label it from source."

"Time!"

"Good, can you feel the separation between you and your sense of time?"

Her body jerked, and she began to breathe deeply. Slowly, a broad grin formed on her face. "This is a preliminary exercise?!"

I took her on through the fifteen initiation steps and into the confidential procedures. It took just over an hour.

I left her sitting in the office smiling and examining a shaft of sunlight on her rolling hand. She was relaxed and her eyes were moist. I was surprised at how extraordinarily beautiful she was.

Each of the next three sessions ended in tears of joy.

In the afternoon I began the same procedure on the fifth volunteer. The session went smoothly at first and then hit an old snag. The person described a persistent condition that she had been trying to handle in therapy for ten years. I listened as the disappointment and failure choked up in her voice.

She is sitting in the middle of a creation.

She told me it would be okay if we just ignored it and handled some minor stuff. She didn't want to ruin my Avatar process with her case. "No," I told her. That was exactly what I was looking for. "Let's explore the persistent condition together and maybe get a little improvement."

She doesn't have a chance of leaving this session with that creation. It's comforting to have the tools to help someone.

We took her old creation apart piece by piece. She was astonished that she didn't have to crab-scuttle through hours of primordial trauma to locate the cause of the condition. "It's right here, isn't it? I'm creating it!" She was amazed by what happened to her when she separated from the resisted experience. "I literally can feel myself change! It's a fantastic process!"

That session ended with the physical condition completely resolved. Her face had changed and she didn't even look like the same person. She was beautiful. She hugged me.

"What have we been doing all these years with therapy? Harry, this is a real breakthrough! I feel like I have just stepped out of the dark ages of my own consciousness. It's hard to believe how fast it works."

After seven more hours, all nine volunteers were through the procedures and were giggling together in the lounge. It had been a remarkable day. One of them sipped a cup of tea, and the others discovered that they could experience the flavor of the tea!

With their individual identities relaxed, they intuitively operated as a team. There was no hint of any divisive self-interest. No conflict. They finished each other's sentences without any sense of interruption or offense. They made sandwiches in a spontaneous assembly-line procedure that would have amazed even Henry Ford. When it was over, knives were washed, everything was put away, the counter was wiped and the sandwiches were on the table. It was fabulous to watch the cooperation. *After all the mental garbage is gone, people cooperate intuitively. What a tool for business!*

People who had not been part of the test group spontaneously gathered around. They experienced a sense of special care from the volunteers. Handshakes turned into hugs and even deliberately repeated hugs. There was a familiar friendliness. *Like old jeans.*

Students arrived for evening classes but never made it beyond the lounge. We declared a holiday. People sat on the stairs and hunched along the walls to listen as the new **Avatars** shared their realizations. The whole atmosphere was electric.

"Whatever you think you are is really only the reflection of you thinking it."

"The illusion is that you are either something or nothing. You are neither."

"Consciousness does not have to operate according to the logic of physical universe laws."

"Judgments are what cause experience to be painful."

"When you allow that others can heal themselves spontaneously, you will be able to heal yourself spontaneously."

"The idea that there is some hard reality that we have to adapt ourselves to and be realistic about is just another form of fear."

"Regret is a break in higher-self trust. You stop trusting that your higher self is creating the experience that it needs for its own evolvement."

The students were fascinated and impatient to ask questions.

"Do you have to remember your past to change your beliefs?" a student asked.

"Only if you believe you do!" said the woman who had handled her persistent condition. "The past is an idea created in the present to serve as an explanation for the judgments we make."

"Will this help me with the upset I have with my wife?"

"It's **your impression** of your wife that you are upset with. Your impression does not depend upon your wife, but on your beliefs. You can change them."

The discussions had a transforming effect on the non-participants. Soon there was no need for questions. Everyone present knew what the answer would be: "What do you believe?"

Personal responsibility made easy! There was a calmness and an expansive, shared viewpoint of existence. Everyone present sensed that a profound shift in consciousness was occurring. There was more hugging.

A sense of a spiritual presence was in the air. It felt like a higher intelligence had been summoned. A new level. An awakening. An ancient set of gears began to move, and a wave of realizations was released into the collective consciousness. What began as an exploration of the mechanics of individual consciousness had opened unexpected doors. A staggering amount of complexity and confusion began to dissolve into simplicity.

It was well after midnight when the gathering broke up. It felt like a historic moment. No one will forget the day of their Avatar initiation.

I was feeling very pleased with myself, but the future tugged at me, reminding me that there was a long road ahead. So this was what destiny felt like. Somehow I intuitively knew that the Avatar seed would grow. It must be cultivated with care. I was happy for what I had accomplished, but at the same time there was a tinge of sadness for the contemplative life that I was leaving behind.

There was no doubt now that humanity was more than a tribe of smart apes. For too long we had lived under a blanket of secrets about our beginnings and our purpose in the universe. And now the truth started to peep out. As I turned off the lights, I had a feeling of connection...a dream **then** and a reality **now,** tied to each other, connecting across millennia. Something that had gone bad had righted itself. A spell was broken. A mid-course correction. A pledge was kept.

Part II:
The Teachings

The Preamble

Before one has studied people for long, it becomes evident that many have forgotten that they are the most sovereign, omniscient creators of their own lives. One sees people who unknowingly create suffering for themselves and then attempt to explain the suffering by electing the universe as cause of it. One sees people who have reduced their own creative power to the bare whispering of a few pleas for mercy from the fear and pain that fill their days.

A milestone in the research of the Avatar materials was the development of a technique that demonstrated that the world one experienced was ultimately shaped by one's consciousness and not the other way around. As it turned out, the technique was also a very effective tool for reshaping both consciousness and experience.

Avatar closed forever the overdue accounts of past therapies and ideologies and confirmed the ageless suspicions about the creative potential of the human spirit!

And now I adopt the conspiratorial whisper of a lover,
for the best I am loves you.
You have done and can do no wrong that I do not share.
Nothing can modify my love for you.
In harmony may the thoughts fashioned here
remind you of what you've always known.
To the canons of man this single line is added:
"Truth is what you create it to be."

By these lines you are introduced to the Creative Path.
You may turn away and embrace the belief systems of others,
but having once heard, the whisper shall never leave thee.

Chapter Eight

The History of Belief Systems

be.lief n.[*BE-* (to be around; edge; boundary; limit) + *-LIEF* (life)]
1. the state of believing; conviction or acceptance that certain things
are true or real **2.** faith, esp., religious faith **3.** trust or confidence (*I
have belief in his ability*) **4.** anything believed or accepted as true;
esp., a creed, doctrine or tenet **5.** an opinion; expectation; judgment
(*my belief is that he'll come*)

SYN. **belief**, the term of broadest application in this comparison,
implies mental acceptance of something as true, even though
absolute certainty may be absent; **faith** implies complete, unques-
tioning acceptance of something even in the absence of proof and,
esp., of something not supported by reason; **trust** implies assurance,
often apparently intuitive, in the reliability of someone or something; **confidence** also suggests such assurance, esp. when based on
reason or evidence; **credence** suggests mere mental acceptance of
something that may have no solid basis in fact

T he history of civilization is the story of the beliefs originated or
adopted by influential individuals. Every political movement,
every religion, every philosophy has its beginning in the confi-
dent expression of a single belief.

This initial belief is probably put forth as a spontaneous comment. The
more attention attracted by it, the more often it is repeated. *Stay away
from the tiger or he might try to eat you.*

When the belief is repeated, it spreads and acquires the status of knowledge. As knowledge, it can be used to support further beliefs. *It's not safe*

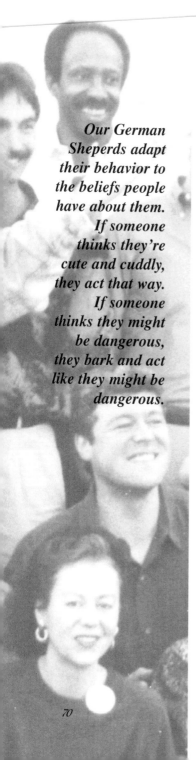

in the jungle. Why? The tiger lives there.

Thus belief systems – bodies of knowledge – arise.

Belief systems appear to be a natural evolutionary process, but do they arise from a situation needing a solution or do they **create** a situation that needs a solution? Is the jungle dangerous because of the tiger or because of the beliefs about tigers? Do the expectations placed upon the tiger communicate a non-verbal suggestion to the tiger as to how he should behave? Is there a behind-the-scenes communication among creatures that choreographs their interactions in accord with some resolution of expectations created by their beliefs?

Unfortunately, before the general population had a chance to ask these questions, someone discovered that belief systems were valuable! As long as people could be made to feel a need for them, they could be traded for food, shelter or safety. HOW-TO-DEAL-WITH-TIGERS (or something analogous to tigers, e.g., snakes, hunger, depression, death, etc.) was a valuable belief system as long as the tiger could be relied upon to fulfill the role of dangerous predator. *Adopting policies of shoot-on-sight helped to eliminate the tame tigers who weren't fulfilling their role.*

Over time, certain individuals, families, tribes and finally even governmental organizations developed a strong vested interest in extolling certain belief systems. In many

Our German Sheperds adapt their behavior to the beliefs people have about them. If someone thinks they're cute and cuddly, they act that way. If someone thinks they might be dangerous, they bark and act like they might be dangerous.

cases the belief system became the basis of the group's economic survival. The sale of belief systems (or the social status obtained from the gift of belief systems) became the founding purpose for great organizations. Proselytizing religions were born. Taxation of the unorganized by the organized appeared. Architecture, art and science evolved in service to the faithful believers.

To ensure that one's organization would survive and prosper, carefully managed balances between "the tigers" and "the solutions to tigers" had to be maintained. Solutions that were too effective required the creation of more challenging, and thus more profitable, problems. New beliefs resulting in diseases, famines and deadly human enemies superseded fear of the tiger.

Wars began. When one group saw the power and influence conveyed to them by their special belief systems eroded by the introduction of competing belief systems, their young men were painfully indoctrinated with the group's beliefs and formed into armies. Any detailed study of history will reveal an initial struggle between beliefs (an argument!), as the fundamental factor for conflicts on this planet.

Wars seldom addressed whose beliefs would create the preferred experiences, but were more a contest to determine whose beliefs (like offspring) would survive. The rightness of a belief was determined by the fierceness of its believers.

The irony of war was that entire civilizations fought to preserve belief systems that resulted in self-oppression and wrought greater self destruction than the deadliest weapons of their enemies. Fascism appeared.

Beliefs were enthroned. Compulsory schooling forcefully indoctrinated entire generations with beliefs. Beliefs grew in importance until they were more valuable than life. Any member who would not fight and risk dying for his group's belief was considered a coward.

There was no equal in inhumanity to the battle fought in the name of the "true belief." No quarter was possible when people fought for a sacred belief. No mercy was shown by or expected from the man who was convinced that his family's honor, his country's honor and perhaps his own soul's salvation was dependent upon the destruction of his "wrongly believing" enemy. The more blood that was spilled asserting a belief, the more sacred and infectious it became for successive generations.

More than once, beliefs about country, about God, and about economic needs have provided the justifications for world wars that have left the civilizations of the victor, as well as of the vanquished, in ashes.

Why? Is there some dark corner in the human mind into which none dare to look? A sinister place of sacred belief? A place where doubt can never be allowed to enter? Some core assumption that none dare utter?

"I know the truth."

* * *

So what is truth? Are there incontrovertible truths? Let's take a closer look at belief systems.

Chapter Nine

Orders of
Belief Systems

TYPE ONE BELIEF SYSTEMS

Type One belief systems depend upon an emotional appeal to fear, sympathy, distrust or hatred. "You'd better believe – or else." Allegiance to Type One belief systems is generally maintained by the introduction of some form of the following two beliefs:

> It is a lack of faith or honor if you doubt the truth of your own belief system.

> If another questions your beliefs, it is a hostile act motivated by evil.

Type One belief systems intentionally cripple the abilities of believers to observe, discern or reason. Members who have doubts are required to make amends by self-damaging acts of contrition or sacrifice.

All but the most emotionally dependent eventually develop an unresponsiveness to

*Examples of Type One beliefs:
(This is how it is.)*

- *You can't trust a _____.*

- *You're going to burn in hell if you don't _____.*

- *You have been victimized by _____.*

- *You're not source because _____ is source.*

the manipulative fear and emotional appeal of Type One systems. Most drift away, often with shame and regret for their former conduct and their own gullibility.

TYPE TWO BELIEF SYSTEMS

Type Two belief systems gain support by appealing to the needs and insecurities of people. They are the tiger cures or belief solutions talked about earlier. Here one finds the logic behind the social customs of a people, the common knowledge that passes without question, the broad collective agreements of what is true. Type Two systems often contain stoic beliefs about the inevitability of suffering.

Examples of Type Two beliefs: (This is how it is.)

• Sometimes you have to do things you don't want to do.

• Certain things just aren't good for you.

• You probably ought to see a doctor.

• Sometimes I'm source and sometimes God is.

Type Two systems are usually transparent (invisible) to their adherents. The beliefs upon which they rest are seldom questioned. The agreements of the members form an invisible doctrine, possibly telepathic in nature, that is experienced as fact. Those who do question the agreements are more likely to be socially outcast or considered insane, rather than scholarly or hostile.

It is common, at least in the last century, for the offspring of those who hold Type Two belief systems to assert their independence by rebelling against their parents' common-sense beliefs. Unfortunately, this often makes them emotionally susceptible to zealous cults promoting Type One belief systems.

Avatar Masters Course
Amsterdam, 1992

TYPE THREE BELIEF SYSTEMS

Type Three belief systems depend upon factual evidence. The believers of Type Three systems generally object to the notion that they are involved with a belief system and prefer to call their belief systems sciences, technologies, or bodies of hard objective fact.

Type Three adherents are frequently addicted to thinking and/or arguing. In order to even consider a viewpoint outside of their particular paradigm, many of them require an environment where judgments are suspended and a strenuous discipline is enforced to still mental processes.

The more able Type Three adherents, who provided the models for aspiring students seeking to escape Type One and Type Two structures, are extremely persuasive and can quote many facts to support the truth of their "objective" belief systems. Type Three believers argue the truth of their beliefs by a heavy reliance on sensory impact (particularly pain), evidence from the past, and logical assumptions.

Their truth, upon examination, is never more than a conviction that certain factors have a greater predictable repeatability than certain other factors. Their basic assumption is that consistent behaviors, whether of people or materials, demonstrate some truth.

Occasionally a Type Three believer experiences a remission of his or her insistence of

Examples of Type Three beliefs:
(This is how it is.)

• *For every action there is an equal and opposite reaction.*
• *Seeing is believing.*
• *It's all a matter of relativity.*
• *Knowledge allows me to be source.*

rightness and, from a new perspective, begins to see that certain facts are really nothing more than the foundational beliefs of a single reality sphere floating in all possibility. It is a moment in which one truely understands paradigms.

This frequently happens to individuals who take the Avatar® course.

TYPE FOUR BELIEF SYSTEMS

Type Four belief systems contain intentionally created beliefs. They are created so that their creators can acquire experiences, new perspectives, and ultimately reassure themselves of their own unlimited source. This is the belief system of gods. Avatar is a Type Four belief system.

Type One, Type Two and Type Three belief systems are various degrees of unawareness of the existence of Type Four belief systems. Type Four belief systems establish the rules and playing fields for the other types.

Type Four belief systems are usually temporary and changeable as there is no hard reality that they pretend to reflect. The Avatar materials contain instructions and tools that one can use to deliberately create, manage and enjoyably experience the many variations of Type Four beliefs.

The adherents of Type Four systems look upon their beliefs, as well as those of others, as the blueprints for experiential reality.

Examples of Type Four beliefs:

(This is how you could make it.)

• *Things always work out for me.*
• *Life teaches me what I need to know.*
•*I intuitively make the right choices.*
• *(Make up your own!)*

Type Four believers employ beliefs to knowingly create in the medium of experience. They believe for the purpose of experiencing. They tend to be appreciative and respectful of different belief systems, but will seldom defend any. They frequently change their beliefs to explore new possibilities and new facets of experience.

What experience would you like to explore?

What would you like to believe?

Chapter Ten

Recovering Your Mental Blueprints

T here is a difference between "exploring" and "searching."

Think back to when you were younger, and you had the opportunity to explore some new terrain or a new experience. You decided where to go and how to proceed. Wasn't it exciting? An adventure! For most people there is a thrill in discovering new places and seeing new things. This is the mental state of an explorer, of a Type Four believer.

Then, something strange happens. You discover that one of your possessions is missing. Maybe a purse or a wallet, a jackknife or a piece of jewelry. Something personal that has value to you. Lost! Was it left behind, or what? You search your memory, then your pockets, and then you start looking around.

You go back over the same terrain, retracing your steps, but now you are in the mental state of a searcher. You look here, trying to remember. You look there, your desperation brings you to the edge of tears. Perhaps you even offer a prayer or two. You quiz yourself: "When did I have it last?" or, "What do I do?"

Now you are lost. Life is no longer an adventure. The thrill and excitement are suppressed by the anguish you feel. There is a filter over your eyes that turns everything into a disappointment. New experiences and potential opportunities present themselves, but they are not what you are looking for.

Even if you succeed in finding the item, the trauma of having lost it may persist. If it does, you stop exploring or searching and begin protecting. Until a person recovers the playfulness of exploring, most of their deliberate actions will be motivated by a desire to find, to protect, or to avoid something.

Beliefs, too, can become lost. How? By becoming so familiar that they are forgotten. It happens after the goal or purpose changes. When the goal was to be cuddled and cared for by mom, the belief, "I'm cute and helpless," was assistive and valuable. One assumed it and it became part of the self. Later when the goal changed, the belief was lost, forgotten. It became transparent. Now, the person perceives and acts through it without being aware that it's there. People lose awareness of what they believe.

The more beliefs that people have to act and perceive through, the harder it is for them to live the way they want to. When they relax, their lives slip into the pattern of the old beliefs, e.g., "I am cute and helpless" – not a very appropriate belief for a top business executive. Lost awareness of beliefs is responsible for stress and self-sabotage. There are many lost beliefs to be found at the bottom of a failing life, a failing relationship or a failing business.

Lost beliefs form an invisible blueprint for feelings and actions, and without understanding why, we create or attract the circumstances that will fulfill them.

Are there beliefs in your blueprint that are no longer of value? They need to be discarded before you can recover the natural high of the explorer. But what are they? How are they found?

How did you get where you are? How did you get yourself into this situation? How do you get out? You try to create a new life, but what happens? It is sabotaged and shattered by lost beliefs. How do you get on with designing your life?

Avatar can help you find the answers.

***

Both *CREATIVISM* and the soon to be released Avatar® workbook, *RESURFACING*, contain exercises that supplement the preceding text. The exercises on transparent beliefs can help you recover the blueprint that underlies your feelings and actions. Like most Avatar exercises, they are simple to understand but require courage and exceptional self-honesty to successfully apply them.

We'll talk about that next.

Chapter Eleven

A Private Talk On Honesty

The ancient Greek philosopher Diogenes is said to have wandered the streets of Athens with a lantern looking for an honest person. Since Diogenes' most remarkable teachings have become known as the Cynic school of philosophy,* I assume that his wanderings were in vain.

Honesty is a very delicate subject to talk about. In most circles, no one would ever be so tactless as to even bring it up. Pirates, criminals, swindlers and con artists proclaim their honesty most loudly. No wonder it has become a subject that tends to besmirch the speaker at its mere mention!

So I am aware that I am walking on the thin ice of the holier-than-thou, but this is an important subject. Without self-honesty, a person will substitute rationalized thinking for his or her genuine feelings. With such, the question, "What do you feel?" will evoke intellectual speculation (*What should I feel?*) rather than an actual experience of what is present.

Dishonest displays of so called "honest" feelings are often intended to deceive , manipulate or to camouflage hidden agendas, for example, *your distrust hurts me deeply.* Treating others dishonestly invariably results in

---

* *The Cynics believe that right actions (courage) and right thinking (self-honesty) are the only things of value. They believe that independence of worldly needs and pleasures brings liberation. They believe that right actions and right thinking are the only things that can save one from wasted lifetimes spent in material pursuits.*

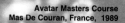

Pretending is imagination without faith.
Creating is imagination with faith.
People who believe in their pretenses create them for real!

a lowering of respect for them. Friends we have discarded, we have first deceived. The same applies to the respect we have for ourselves and our lost selves. Dishonesty is at the root of asserted self-importance.

We seem able to lie easily about our own honesty. Some part of us automatically insists that we are honest without even inspecting what we are doing or saying. Catch children in the act and more than likely the first words out of their mouths will be, "I didn't do it!"

It seems easier to defend actions than to honestly examine them. We are quicker to attack than admit. Admissions require courage!

Being honest is really a question of courage – courage enough to face what we fear. This gets lost in the smoke screen of deceptions that is used to justify dishonesty. Whenever we accept that there is good reason to be dishonest – hardship, desperation, depression, ignorance, victimhood, etc. – we increase the evidence for fearing what we are avoiding. And what is it? Only this: **fear is a BELIEF in our inadequacy to deal with something.** And that belief precedes any evidence of failure we have collected!

So, do we have the courage to face what we fear? This is life's most severe test – failure leads to unawareness.

Unawareness arising from fear is why people are dishonest. The belief responsible for the fear may be lost in confusion or hidden in the shame of humiliation. The invitation is to avoid, to forget, to go stupid, and the urge to be right further sanctions our ignorance.

What a breath of fresh air to face a dishonest act and say, "I did it because I was afraid. Period!" That is the first step toward discovering the hidden fear. What a relief! There is no longer a need to struggle to change the world or circumstances or anybody else! You can work on yourself. You need only to gather your courage and look for a **BELIEF** you have about your own inadequacy! At the bottom of every dishonest act, there is at least one.

Here is a remarkable observation that has profound implications for the future of the world: *as people handle their transparent and hidden beliefs, they become naturally more honest!*

> **cour.age** n. the attitude of facing and dealing with anything recognized as dangerous, difficult, or painful, instead of withdrawing from it
>
> **in.ad.e.qua.cy** n. not equal to what is required or considered sufficient
>
> **pre.tend** vt. an effort to experience or display something different from what one feels or believes (in regard to self, others or events)

Deliberate pretending is an acting skill and shouldn't be confused with compulsive pretending-motivated-by-fear, which is a specialized form of dishonesty that masks one's intentions. The following observations apply to compulsive pretending.

Compulsive pretending soaks up one's attention and consumes creative energies. Compulsive pretending destroys motivation and displaces intuition. Compulsive pretending reduces one's ability to operate harmoniously in the world. Compulsive pretending creates an internal stress that seeks an outlet. Sometimes the result is disease, sometimes violence.

Eventually, compulsive pretense deadens the ability to deal honestly with others or to be honest with oneself. Every time one is reminded (or accused) of pretending, the response is to become defensive and critical. Eventually one loses touch with his or her genuine feelings. Pretenders create false identities that are staged, egocentric and insensitive.

Pretenders criticize, gossip about and covertly attack people whose honesty reminds them of their own pretenses; eventually this becomes a compulsive behavior pattern. They assume that everyone else is also pretending, so their attacks specialize in exposé.

Pretenders are good people frightened into bad actions. They operate on hidden agendas. To lessen their sense of guilt, they project on to others identities that deserve to be cheated, swindled, robbed, lied about, deceived or defrauded in some way. Most of the definitive catalogs describing the antisocial, criminal minds, sinners, etc., are the compilations of pretenders. (It is a sensible wisdom to view the accuser with some suspicion.)

People who cannot trust themselves become the fugitives of society. They punish themselves indirectly by putting their trust in the people who are least likely to return it. Then they parade the fact that they have been betrayed. This eases their own burden. In place of personal integrity, they rely on the grand absolution of sin: *everybody does it!* Their personal lives are a whirlpool of bad relationships and failed projects. In the end, pretense strengthens the fear it was meant to conceal.

In the end, pretense strengthens the fear it was meant to conceal.

You have done and can do no wrong
I do not share.

* * *

As disagreeable as it may be to contemplate, the dishonesty I encounter in the world is a reflection of my own pretense. Pretending that I am honest and that others are not doesn't work. That is the trap that awaits those who will not assume ownership for the world's dishonesty.

We are all dishonest as long as we do not compassionately work to correct the collective dishonesty of the world. How? Punishments and threats of exposure are poor answers. A better answer is for each of us, in our personal lives and our dealings with others, to set a courageous example of honesty – even when it means exposing ourselves to the criticism and judgments of pretenders.

Honesty is a path that leads to happiness. Becoming honest is an act of self renewal.

When we summon the courage to take ownership of our experiences, to see them just as they are, to feel them, we will recover the blueprints of our lives. We will face our fears and find the transparent beliefs that create them. Becoming more honest with ourselves means introducing more honesty into the collective consciousness of the world, and this lays a foundation upon which an enlightened planetary civilization can be built.

The result of living honestly is feeling and sharing – compassion and empathy! There

Avatar Masters Course
La Napole, France, 1990

Some key questions:

"Do my words and actions add to the collective honesty in the world or to the collective dishonesty?"

"Would I like living in a world where everyone is as honest as I am?"

is a joy in willingly integrating with the consciousness of others. Attention and creative energies combine with a synergetic result. Networking and new opportunities present themselves. Relationships develop that are rewarding and provide a measure of security that no amount of money, power or fame can provide. Valid trust arises.

Chapter Twelve

Viewpoint and The Nature of Being

"We know only what we experience. Does what we experience reflect some solid immutable reality?...We know only what we experience."

–Avatar lecture, 1988

cre.ate *vt.* [from Latin creare, to make] **1.** to cause to come into existence; bring into being; make; originate; esp., to make or design **2.** to bring about; give rise to; cause

de.fine vt. [from Latin *definire,* to limit] **1.** *a)* to determine or set down the boundaries of *b)* to trace the precise outline of; delineate **2.** to determine or state the extent and nature of; describe exactly *(define* your duties) **3.** *a)* to give the distinguishing characteristics of *b)* to constitute the distinction of; differentiate *(reason *defines* man)* **4.** to state the meaning or meanings of (a word, etc.)

The universe consists of awareness defining itself. All-that-is is all that is. Dividing it up and parceling it out is the role of creation.

Viewpoint: the point from which something is viewed

A belief has definition and dimension in consciousness. Believing **creates** the belief. Believing is the conscious part of creating.

Beliefs have the capacity to stimulate impressions, to filter impressions or to react with other creations.

Some beliefs contain viewpoints. When a belief contains a viewpoint it is called a self. The identity, or personality, of the self is formed by the characteristics of the belief occupied. The more defined the belief, the more defined the identity. The more flexible the belief, the more flexible the identity.

Behind viewpoint is the timeless, spaceless massless, energyless awareness that underlies all creation. It perceives by becoming the thing perceived. In this mode of perception there is no separation between the perceiver and the perception. Perception is the same as being. And awareness can be anything.

Realities extend outward from viewpoints. Viewpoints and realities interact to produce the phenomena of energy, space and time.

***

***

A new reality may be defined by a viewpoint already existing within a prior reality. But, if we wish to preserve order, realities defined within existing realities must respect the limitations of the host reality.

An initial unreality (disorder) occurs when one creates a new reality that violates the limits of the host reality. Persevering through this unreality is essential to expansion and growth.

***

Two things that are alike in all respects, are they not the same? Ultimate reality has no definitions, limits or boundaries. Pure awareness has no definition, limits or boundaries.

Existence is a cycle that begins with believing and concludes with experiencing.

Many viewpoints may exist simultaneously within a single reality. The viewpoints may or may not agree upon their interpretation of the reality; thus many interpreted realities may exist within the shared reality.

Generally, more expansive states of consciousness are source for less expansive states. Viewpoints operate as limited source, creations within creations.

***

The structure and mechanics of the physical universe may be extrapolated from these ideas.

Many interpreted realities may exist within the shared reality.

Avatar Masters Course
Elmira, New York, 1989

Chapter Thirteen

The Great Divide

I n an effort to categorize reality, some viewpoint constructs the idea of an "inside reality" and an "outside reality" and creates a mind to decide what belongs where. Thereafter, what is perceived as outside the mind is objective reality, and what is perceived inside the mind (apperceived) is subjective reality.

This separation of reality into the objective (physical) and the subjective (mental) leads to the assumption (belief) that what is in the mind is consciousness and what is outside the mind is something else – a mystery. This permits the construction of a reality that appears to be independent of the perceiver.

The next step in the grand illusion is to conclude that consciousness is the result of man's interaction with this independent physical reality. What an effective trap this makes! A mystery is created and then the mystery becomes the source of the mystery's creator!

The trap tells us that we determine what we believe from our experience of previously defined realities. Thus we continuously shrink and solidify the creation in which we

Consciousness does not evolve from the universe; the universe evolves from consciousness.

operate. The result is a being in a very defined, solid sphere of reality (e.g., the physical universe).

Anyway, a pretty neat creation, this mind thing, except that once it is programmed by physical reality, it reduces one's power to create reality. It thereafter filters the creation of realities through what it has already experienced. One no longer perceives a chair, but now perceives mother's favorite chair that she loved to sit in on Sundays and visit with Aunt Agnes, or that grandmother rocked in while she knitted, or the chair that father bought at the auction.

Thus reality becomes a personal interpretation having more to do with what was created than what is created. Memories and perception begin to merge into beliefs about reality. This leads to the notion that all reality is a product of prior realities that are products of prior realities etc., which leaves us with psychotherapy and Dianetics. *I'm afraid of cats because I was scratched by one when I was a baby. The past is responsible for the present. I am created by what I already created.* Behold, the grand illusion!

But wait! Stop! Dead-end! The point is missed: **what is considered objective NOW is the result of subjective speculation NOW!**

So it's all defined awareness – consciousness! A holographic matrix that supports specialized impressions, one of which is called objective reality, one of which is called subjective reality. Without awareness the questions of subjectivity and objectivity do not arise.

It's all defined awareness.

Chapter Fourteen

Creativism and Reality

"I call my philosophy Creativism because it is not discovered truth, it is created truth. Most philosophies are derived from some fundamental experience or understanding of the universe – not Creativism; it is created by awareness at source. It contains the minimal tools that one needs to self-determinedly navigate in the realm of consciousness. This is the path of Avatar."

–Avatar lecture, 1988

Consciousness does not evolve from the universe; the universe evolves from consciousness.

ex.pe.ri.ence n. [*ex-* out + *peri-*, to attempt, venture] **1.** the act of living through an event or events; personal involvement in or observation of events **as they occur 2.** anything observed or lived through *(*an *experience* he'll never forget) **3.** *a)* all that has happened to one in his life to date *(*not within his *experience) b)* everything done or undergone by a group, people in general, etc.

4. effect on a person of anything or everything that has happened to him; individual reaction to events, feelings, etc. **5.** *a)* activity that includes training, observation or practice, and personal participation *b)* the period of such activity *c)* knowledge, skill, or practice resulting from this—**vt. -enced, -enc.ing** to have experience of; personally encounter or feel; meet with; undergo

Believing defines realities; experiencing dissolves realities. This is the cycle of creation.

Reality is now and it begins and ends with you!

Creation begins with a statement (primary belief) that defines a reality. The reality is then (or later) experienced by the creator. The interval between the expression of the primary belief and the conclusion of the experience defines time.

As long as a creator **voluntarily** owns and appreciates his or her creation, the action of creating is ongoing. When appreciated, the creation returns to the awareness from which it came. But when a creator disowns his or her creation (through lapse of memory, denial, judgment, invalidation, etc.), and refuses to experience it, the substance and form of the creation persists.

The reason a creator fails to appreciate a creation is because, in the interval between origination and experience, the creator experiences a change of viewpoint. From the new viewpoint, the creation doesn't appear as something one would logically create. Until the old viewpoint is reassumed, ownership is denied. The new viewpoint reacts against the original creation by originating new layers of beliefs which are experienced either as delight or resistance to the original creation. These additional layers create the experiences of what is ugly and what is beautiful, what is right and what is wrong, and what is appropriate and what is inappro-

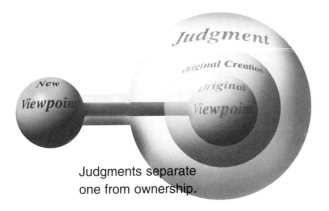

Judgments separate
one from ownership.

Avatar Masters Course
Geneva Switzerland, 1993

priate. These additional layers create the experience of opinions and judgments about the original creation.

Opinions and judgments separate one further from ownership and experience of the original creation. Thus the original creation, not being owned and appreciated, persists by default.

All of the confusion and random events in our lives occur because of these changes in viewpoint. Forgetfulness, as an example, occurs after a change in viewpoint. We originate a belief we want to experience, but because our mind is agitated, before we experience it we shift our viewpoint, change our mind and originate a new belief. Now we are "believing over" our original beliefs. Reality over reality. What do we experience? A little of this and a little of that, confusion and random events.

The quintessential viewpoint, which we have forgotten, is that of the primal universal Creator.

The quintessential viewpoint, which we have forgotten, is that of the primal universal Creator.

Imagine no boundaries...

So the first step back to that viewpoint is to accept that where we are is exactly and only where we are. To begin the process of sorting out our lives, we must own and appreciate the circumstances we find ourselves in right now – continuously.

Realize that in this present moment we are exactly where we once decided we wanted to be. There is no point in second-guessing the wisdom behind our decision. It made sense at the time. When we assume responsibility for our lives, we will begin to appreciate the wisdom of all our creations, and we will find in them empowering lessons. As we learn, the solidity of our reality will begin to soften and dissolve, layer by layer, until we behold the core beliefs that created it.

Now we know what really powerful creators we are. And with the Avatar tools we can operate from that space where we can change our beliefs to shape the next moment. This is the art of living deliberately.

As our judgments and resistances are dissolved and our stillness of mind deepens, we recover the ability to experience the foundational beliefs that create all reality.

The path is clearly marked. When whatever condition we find ourselves in is experienced, the next level of beliefs will show up. When that level is experienced, the next appears, etc. Beliefs show up in the following order:

- beliefs that create conditions in our life
- beliefs about requirements and obligations
- beliefs about responsibility and ownership
- beliefs that create identities
- beliefs that create time
- beliefs defining the nature of matter
- beliefs defining the behavior of energy
- beliefs that create space

Chapter Fifteen

Designing Our Own Reality

de.cide vt. [*de-*, off, from + *caedere* to cut] **1.** to end (a contest, dispute, etc.) by giving one side the victory or by passing judgment **2.** to make up one's mind or reach a decision about; determine (to *decide* which tie to wear) **3.** to cause to reach a decision

SYN. decide implies the bringing to an end of vacillation, doubt, dispute, etc., by making up one's mind as to an action, course, or judgment; **determine** in addition suggests that the form, character, functions, scope, etc., of something are precisely fixed (the club *decided* on a lecture series and appointed a committee to *determine* the speakers, the dates, etc.); **settle** stresses finality in a decision, often one arrived at by arbitration, and implies the termination of all doubt or controversy; **to conclude** is to decide after careful investigation or reasoning; **resolve** implies firmness of intention to carry through a decision (he *resolved* to go to bed early every night)

–Webster's New World Dictionary

Given enough time, everyone will become aware that what they believe has a direct consequence on their lives. Unfortunately, most children do not get this discovery time and are bombarded from an early age by what they **should** believe. The result is that what they sometimes **say** they believe (their indoctrination) obscures what they truly believe.

The real dilemma of existence is deciding **what** to believe. Entire lifetimes are spent side-stepping this decision. The majority of us are already deeply patterned and indoctrinated by the time we realize that deciding for ourselves is an option. Deciding is fundamental to creating!

Eventually we learn that the beliefs we truly hold, the ones we've **decided** to believe, our **faith**, will cause us to create or attract experiences which will verify them. The beliefs we have merely accepted as part of our indoctrination may sustain an existing reality, but they will never create a new one.

Reality consists of the experiences we believe are real. What is real may or may not be the same for everyone.

Fantasies are the experiences we believe are not real.

Pretending is resisting what we decided to believe.

Doubt is a conflict between new decisions and old decisions.

What we believe and how we believe determine our reality.

To make something real we must believe in it/ For it to be real to others, they must believe in it./To the degree that we fail to manage our beliefs, reality will remain beyond our control.

* * *

We experience what we believe. If we don't believe that we experience what we believe, then we don't, which still means the first statement is true.

We may believe that what we experience will surprise us, which then it usually does./ We may believe the experience will enlighten us, which then it probably will. We may believe we will have to look long and hard to find the experience... We may believe we will never find the experience... We may believe there is no experience to find... We may believe there is nothing we can do about it, even if we find the experience... We may believe the experience we find is not the experience we believed we would find... We may believe anything we please, and when we decide to believe it without doubt, it is what we will experience as reality.

So, from the viewpoint of source, any perception or creation, directly or indirectly received through any sensory channel, through the imagination, through intuition, through faith – through any dimension – can be experienced as real or not, dependent only upon what we deliberately believe. (It is not possible to have a perception or creation that does not exist, but one may believe the perception or creation is unreal. Human beings intentionally limit their own perceptions.)

Thus **reality is anything we believe it to be!** (As long as there is no conflict with our previous beliefs.)

The only thing outside of reality is the inexpressible source. And it is an illusion created by language that there appears to be an inside and an outside. More accurately, if somewhat enigmatically, source occupies an alogical dimension that permeates everything!

Source is awareness without definition. It does not contain separation nor is it contained. There is no difference between what is believed, what is experienced and what is experiencing. Awareness without definition is a unity from which reality arises. The essential self that we experience ourselves to be exists as a creation within this awareness-without-definition. The minimum equation for each of us is: awareness + primal creation = essential self. Essential self is generally expressed as "I am."

Identity is composed of and defined by the additional layers of beliefs that are added to our essential self!

* * *

When people move away from being the source of their beliefs, their past takes over as the source of their beliefs. Responsibility is being source right now. Blame is looking for who was source. People can become addicted to the past to provide answers. Reversing the flow and having a person give answers to the past can be a powerful transformational process.

For a very long time people have weighed evidence, analyzed, and taken measurements to answer, "What should I believe?" It's now clear that this was the wrong question. The right question is, "What do I want to believe?"

* * *

Examples of beliefs:

- I think I might be right.

- Cats are creatures.

- I feel awful because I ate too much.

- You have to pay your dues.

- It's terrible to be sick.

- I am a tolerant person.

- I get sick easily.

- It's hard to earn money.

- Money comes to me easily.

- I am afraid to love.

- It's hard for me to change.

- I'm always late.

- It's difficult because...

- I did my best.

- I'm (I'm not) a nice person.

- It's not that easy.

- You have to be realistic.

- It wouldn't work for me.

- I do what I can.

- I didn't do it.

- I am happy.

- It doesn't matter what I believe.

- Sometimes things just happen.

- Kids are like that.

- Governments are bad.

- I don't have any confidence in authority.

- Everything is a belief.

- There is something more fundamental than belief.

- Somethings can't be changed.

- Everything can be changed.

- It's better to live in the North.

- It's better to live in the South.

- Some things are worth fighting for.

- Nothing is worth fighting for.

- It doesn't matter what I believe.

- One person can't make a difference.

- Everyone makes a difference.

- There is a difference between truth and belief.

- There is no difference between truth and belief.

- I can't afford Avatar.

- There is nothing I can (can't) do.

- This is the way it is.

Chapter Sixteen

Relative Truth and Existence

"Two philosophers in a library walk down a narrow row of bookshelves. At the end of the row, the first philosopher comments on the books he has seen.

'What?' says the second philosopher. 'They are not what I saw.'

They quickly enter into an argument. Why?

Oh, did I mention one philosopher is a foot shorter than the other?"

* * *

"What you observe AS affects what you perceive as true. What you operate AS affects what you can do. Inconsistencies in observation and abilities arise as a result of differences in AS..."

Avatar Wizard lecture, 1991

Things that we say are true about one level of existence may not be true at another level of existence. Things that we view as true from one perspective may not be true from another perspective. Most disagreements and conflicts, particularly in religion, philosophy and psychology, are due **not so much to what is viewed as to a mismatch of viewing levels or perspectives.**

Practices and procedures that transform lives at one level of existence may be unworkable or have no effect at another level of existence.

Knowing the frame of reference of the observer is essential to evaluating the truth of an observation. Drunks sometimes do see pink rabbits!

Since the belief management procedures of Avatar directly address the consciousness that uses them, they are self-adapting to the level of existence being experienced by the person.

The following chart describes four broad levels of existence, the principle concerns of each level, and the results of believing at each level.

Level of Existence	Principal Concerns	Results of Believing
Awareness (Definitionless)	Creating and discreating reality	Believing results in effortless manifestation
Consciousness (Defining)	Thoughts, observations and impressions	Believing results either in a creation or a restimulation of previous creation
Identity (Defined)	Evaluations, preferences and judgments	Believing filters perception
Body (Creation)	Stimulation, regeneration and procreation	Believing aligns (true) or conflicts (false) with an existing reality

Organizing what we determine existence to be into more specific categories, or levels, can be easily done. We can define and categorize existence by the **impact or certainty** with which we perceive it (body level), by the **agreement or desire** expressed by other points of view (identity level), or by the **system or method** by which it is perceived (consciousness level). We can talk about personal realities, sensory realities or conceptual realities, about similarities and differences, but in the final analysis, whenever we talk about any level of existence, we will be talking about the result of our beliefs.

Beliefs are the colored lenses that filter out from all-that-is what we wish to experience.

The human body is a product of beliefs. DNA is a product of beliefs. Together they create a marvelous combination of belief-lenses that filter the impact of certain particles and energies into meaningful frequencies that we experience as physical reality. The human eye registers certain frequencies of light, the ears are tuned to certain thresholds of vibration, etc. And even though we can create wonderful instruments capable of sensing vibratory frequencies beyond the body's tuned filters, they operate only by translating what the body doesn't register into the narrow range of perception that the body can register. The realities not translated are lost to anyone who believes himself or herself as capable of only perceiving within the existence level of a body.

Similar extended capabilities and limitations exist for the identity and consciousness levels of existence.

Prior to experiencing Avatar, many people believe that purely conceptual events such as telepathy, hunches, déjà vu, intuition and other extrasensory perceptions are beyond the limits of their experience. Avatar shows people how to change their level of existence and thus these limiting beliefs. They recognize they are free to explore the endless possibility.

We create possibility by believing ourselves into it, and we dissolve limitation by experiencing ourselves out of it.

***

The universe arises within awareness, not the other way around.

– Avatar Lecture, 1987

Individuals sharing the same belief, whether created or indoctrinated, form a collective consciousness that can define and shape the world.

The events that make up world reality result from a belief blueprint that is continuously redrawn from the vectoring sum of every belief held by every individual. The collective reality is the average of all intention.

Just as adding a single drop to the ocean causes microscopic changes in the volume, the temperature and the currents, every time an individual changes his or her belief, the blueprint by which the collective reality unfolds changes. Even for the most isolated individual, every moment of happiness, every moment of sadness, every kindness, every critical thought adds its consequence to the blueprint for the events of the world.

Tomorrow unfolds in accordance with the intention of our collective beliefs. There will always be as much conflict and suffering in the world as there is ignorance and intolerance in the consciousness of humanity.

The mission of Avatar in the world is to catalyze the integration of belief systems. When we perceive that the only difference between any of us is beliefs, and that beliefs can be created or discreated with ease, the right and wrong game will wind down, and world peace will ensue.

Part III:
The Path

Chapter Seventeen

Expansion

Summer, 1987. Six months after the first Avatars, my wife Avra and I were invited to California to deliver the first west coast Avatar class. There were supposed to be eleven people waiting to enroll in the class, but just before we arrived I learned that none had actually paid. All were waiting to hear me speak before they made their final decision. This was a surprise to me, because I had not prepared anything to say.

More surprises came at the airport. Our luggage was still in Pittsburgh, and our friend who picked us up told us that in addition to the eleven probable students, there were another fifty people waiting at his house to hear me speak. *What am I going to say?*

So, dirty, sweaty and tired, I found myself perched on a stool in a California living room with sixty strangers sitting on the floor around me. If the Avatar processes ever worked, they had to now. I closed my eyes and spent a minute handling my own doubts and nervousness. When I applied the processes, all the doubts slipped away. When I opened my eyes, I was definitionless awareness. *How are you my friends? Have I got a treat for you!*

"I will try to describe Avatar without conveying too many of my own beliefs or perspectives to you. The reason I say that is because the Avatar course is about **your** beliefs and **your** perspectives."

Absolute motionless silence! Sixty people, two babies and a dog, and you could hear the clock on the kitchen wall tick! It was so quiet that it finally unnerved the dog and he surprised himself with a muffled bark. I felt I had said enough. *They know. Let them feel me! Underneath the beliefs, we're part of the same awareness. Feel it.*

The room relaxed as the fog of thoughts cleared. We had touched some-place behind it all and now were friends. We were in love. Eyes filled with tears. Gentle, accepting smiles. *I love this feeling. We're real. The costumes are off and we're real. Together, part of a greater shared destiny.*

"What you believe has consequences in your life. The Avatar course helps you to make the connection between what you are experiencing and the belief that is creating the experience.

"Imagine enrolling on a course where the study materials consist of your own consciousness. We provide navigational tools, a blank map and emotional support. It's your exploration; you have to bring your own terrain.

"The purpose is to assist you in returning to the level of consciousness at which you are the knowing creative source of your own beliefs. Along the way you are going to learn that what you believe is not nearly as important as knowing how you believe. In this case, understanding the container is more important that understanding the contents. Empty the contents! Marvel at the craft that creates the bowl.

"Creative source is an effortless state of being. Don't confuse it with an attitude or identity that may be on automatic and seem effortless. This state is effortless, accepting and undefined. (Desiring and resisting are efforts. Accepting and appreciating are effortless.) From this state of being, you can experience anything and within extremely broad limits (perhaps boundless) change it as you decide.

"This is the state of being that we call Avatar, and we have found a very simple and very effective procedure for achieving this state. It can be done in a matter of days when presented under the guidance of an experienced master. With this sense of presence and the tools we teach you to use, you are equipped for the exploration of your own consciousness."

"The course is set up in three sections. Section I is for the intellect. It's food for thought. It requires only that you listen, read, or watch and if you wish, contemplate what you have experienced. It is intended to bring about an understanding and a connection with a broader arena of life.

"Then with the Section II materials, you start exploring. Little expeditions into the backyard of your consciousness. Overnights! You practice the specific abilities and tools that are required to successfully manage what you are already experiencing in life. It's an opportunity to get your affairs in order before the big adventure begins.

"Section II clarifies and expands an extra-sensory perception channel to the physical universe that you may already be vaguely aware of – extended feeling. This is a non-sensory feeling that does not require physical contact. It quiets the mind and dramatically enhances your sense of being."

A hand goes up in the audience. "Is it like meditation?"

"Yes and no. It produces the same type of mental stillness that meditation produces, but it does so in an interesting and much faster way. It's like meditation in that it is about gaining mastery of the mind – allowing the mind to still – but Avatar does it playfully without the struggle or confrontation. It's the difference between opening a safe by prying the door off or using the combination. Avatar is the combination."

The group likes the analogy. Many of them have spent a lot of time prying.

"Another exercise in Section II develops a skill in recognizing, creating and changing judgments. This really begins to wake you up to the patterns in your life.

"We experience what we experience in accordance with our judgments, which are the beliefs through which we filter our perceptions. Two people may experience the same event quite differently. For one of them it is traumatic and ruins their life; for the other it is inconsequential. The difference is determined by the judgments the two people place on the experience.

"The end result of this exercise is the ability to honestly relax judgment on anything being experienced. It lets you slip into your resisted experiences like entering a hot tub for a good soak. If you have been struggling with a body condition or a relationship, this exercise produces powerful realizations and turning-point experiences.

"The final part of the Section II materials contain tools and exercises to remove barriers or blocks that you may have placed in front of your ability to create reality. We describe it as 'the most challenging experience anyone ever laughed through.' It causes smile cramps in your face, increases your ability to create, and restores your control over existence."

In my mind I see the smiling faces of the students who have thanked me after completing this exercise. Their moist eyes occupy a special place in my memory. I also remember, somewhat sadly, the angry face of one student who didn't make it and denounced Avatar as a fraud. He was frozen at the controls of a failing life and couldn't let go of his righteous anger. *Oh well, when it no longer serves him to be a victim , time will bring him back. Just a little more effort, a little more honesty, and he will make it too.*

In case there are chronic victims present, I feel a little warning is in order.

"If you are not completely satisfied with the results you achieve in Section II, don't go on to Section III. There's nothing in Section III that fixes poor results in Section II. If you don't go on and you decide within the next week or so that Section II wasn't worth what you paid, I'll see to it personally that you get a refund check." I smile to myself. *Has anyone ever offered enlightenment with a money-back guarantee?*

"So now, Section III, the main course. Section III begins with a guided initiation session conducted by an Avatar Master. *"That's me until the new masters are finished with their training.*

"The initiation takes you on a tour of some of the most fundamental, transparent belief structures of consciousness. Transparent, because instead of seeing them, you see through them. The initiation experientially introduces you to procedures and tools that you can use to self-determinedly manage your life. Normally, it is an insightful and enlightening experience and may leave you in a euphoric state for some time."

I'll be surprised if they're not totally blissed out and euphoric for the rest of the day, but I don't say that.

"Following your initiation you will become an expert on the solo Avatar procedures. Now you are ready to explore. With the solo procedures, and the occasional assistance of a trainer or fellow student, you begin your exploration with the **Avatar rundowns.** Each rundown addresses an area of experiences, beliefs or attitudes that may be interfering with your appreciation of life. I'll go over the rundowns for you."

Body Handle Rundown "The first rundown is called Body Handle. The Body Handle processes produce effects similar to sensory deprivation tanking, but without the risk of isolation or panic reactions and much more quickly. They assist you in recognizing the beliefs that keep you identified with a physical body, and if you choose, show you how to function independently of a body. You experience yourself as a non-material spiritual being."

A couple in the front row look at each other knowingly, and I realize they've just made the decision to sign up.

"Body Handle also helps you to identify undesirable perceptions and sensations that you have actually been installing in the body – the illusion was that they were coming from the body. The result is that the body is no longer held out of alignment by injurious beliefs or judgments.

"Once you recognize and experience that you've been installing unpleasant sensations in the body, you can put back the sensations you wish to have. You may experience some remarkable healings." *Remarkable – I've seen miracles, but I don't want trouble with the AMA.*

"A fascinating, side effect of the Body Handle is the lucid, or controlled, dreaming that it produces. You learn to enter the dream state of consciousness without going to sleep. Some students have reported experiences of floating or flying and of exploring alternate dimensions."

Limitations Rundown "The second rundown is called Limitations. Have you ever explored any sort of spiritual or developmental path?" Most raise their hands. "Then you are aware that we set limitations on ourselves. We say, 'I can't do this. . . I can't do that,' and then we wonder why we can't do it.

"Children's stories talk about the little steam engine that 'thought he could' and the notion of 'positive thinking' has been around for years. Well, this is a new look at the subject.

"On the Limitations rundown, you eliminate specific limitations that interfere with the goals that excite you and bring you to life. You will probably not choose to handle all limitations, since some serve to focus your life."

Identities Rundown "The third rundown is called Identities. Most people have a mental closet full of costumes that they carry around and project onto the people they meet. 'Will you wear this costume for me?' 'Will you be this person for me?'

"When we get along well with people, it is generally because they are willing to wear the costume we offer them, and we are willing to wear one supplied by them.

"Have you ever had someone put an identity on you that you didn't want to wear?" This brings nods of agreement from the group.

"When you perceive another person without any costumes, judgments or belief filters, you perceive them as a spiritual being. It is a profoundly moving experience to purely perceive another being without any distortion. It is a compassionate space that some have called unconditional love."

Persistent Mass Handle Rundown   "The fourth rundown is called Persistent Mass Handle. It gently guides you into the most resisted aspects of your life. You can eliminate desires, compulsions, persistent pressures and pains that may have seemed beyond your control. The first sessions of Persistent Mass are done with another person acting as a facilitator. This is a very powerful process and produces amazing life-changing results. "

Universe Handle & Collective Consciousness Handle Rundowns "The fifth and sixth rundowns are called respectively Universe Handle and Collective Consciousness Handle. You do these rundowns after you have resolved your own personal conflicts and wish to help the collective consciousness of life.

"One of the ideas one creates early in life is the idea of being someone. In fact, being someone is the experience of a belief. If you take awareness plus a belief about being someone and put them together, you get an individual. You can stay an individual by creating more beliefs that separate you further from collective consciousness – or with the Avatar procedures, you can eliminate the beliefs that cause separation, and experience a collective consciousness. You can change any beliefs that you may have that separate you from pure creative awareness – the **Aware Will**.

"In the Universe Handle process, you learn that all things are connected at some level of consciousness. In a sense, there is no individual consciousness, only segments of collective consciousness. With this exercise, you work on locating the limits that prevent you from joining the collective consciousness and operating within it.

"This obviously is a very high state of attainment, and students will vary in their ability and willingness to employ this technique."

The Ultimate Process "The last exercise is named The Ultimate Process. It is aptly named. It is guided by another person.

"The whole course takes between seven and nine days, depending upon you."

I ended the talk by inviting people to reach out and feel me, not with their hands but with their awareness.

Everyone in the room seemed interested. I chatted with some friends and felt relief to see a line of students form in front of Avra's registration table. The next day we began class with eighteen new students!

Within a few days the class grew so large with new arrivals that we had to move to a hotel, and our one week west coast delivery stretched into twelve weeks and several hundred students!

Old friends called each other with the message: "This is it! Come now!" One student arrived after hearing about Avatar from a phone call intended for his roommate. Another student received a psychic reading in which she was told to do Avatar. A third arrived because of a dream.

Because so many likened the experience of Avatar to waking up, they began to refer to themselves as Awakening Masters (AM's). Awakening Masters sent out a long-awaited wake-up call. "Avatar is what you are looking for."

The students continued to arrive, even following us back to New York to finish the course.*

I wonder how many of them felt the same as I had the night the green Dodge drew me into Cubbly Park.

---

* *Between 1987 and 1993, approximately 25,000 people completed the Avatar course.*

Chapter Eighteen
The New Civilization

The following is edited from a Master course graduation commencement address given by Harry Palmer, President of Star's Edge International, April 28,1990, in Nice, France

P*icture 250 individuals from 12 countries that for more than a week have lived together at a depth of being that primarily experiences compassion, appreciation and joy. They've come to learn to deliver Avatar and pass the light to others.*

...you've come a long way, you still have a long way to go. The world is changing. Hope is awakening, It is a good time to be alive. It is a good time for noble deeds and sharing humanitarian endeavors. For the first time ever, you have the means and the tools to create a new civilization. That's your gift.

Delusions of grandeur are delusory only as long as they remain unaccomplished. Otherwise they are great and noble deeds. Your will determines now how the future will perceive these days: deluded by grandeur or founders of an enlightened planetary civilization! It's in your hands.

Tomorrow is graduation. I trust you have found the last nine days enlightening.

You should know that you are joining a very powerful worldwide network of the most able beings on this planet. So that you are fully informed before you make this commitment, I want to tell you what the Avatar network stands for and what it stands against.

It is not unusual for men and women to fervently pursue some great cause, to embrace some grand idea of righteousness and to put all their strength and their hearts into banishing some real or imagined wrong ...not unusual for some individual or group to proclaim that they are the virtuous enforcers of a divine teaching and to believe that their scorn and condemnation of evil will save the world. Not unusual. Not at all! But it is also, after five thousand years of failure, clearly unworkable.

Anyone can decide their ideas are righteous. Any idea can be dressed up to look righteous. Righteous ideas are inscribed upon parchment and in holy books. Eventually they become slogans on battle flags that are used to justify insensitive acts for which no individual would ever assume personal responsibility. If they did, they would be tried and convicted for murder! So young men die by the thousands with righteous ideas on every side.

This is the path that you do not stand for. It is better that you denounce Avatar a thousand times than use it even once to justify your actions. You champion no cause above personal responsibility.

As a member of the Avatar network, you work in the world, but you stand outside of it. You now know that you are here by choice and with a mission. You are world redeemers. You are the wake-up crew. You understand that the problems of the world must ultimately be solved where they began – in consciousness.

You work toward the integration that will permit the discreation of every border, every definition of race, every jail and every lock. You work toward an enlightened planetary civilization.

It is your choice and your privilege to live at this time and to witness the progress of Avatar in the world. You have the possibility of achieving in your lifetime more planetary harmony than has ever before existed.

When enough people are able to see that the only real differences between any of us are the ideas and beliefs that we create, there will be a spontaneous worldwide awakening to the fact that we share an inseparable destiny.
As your true nature is realized – undefined and ever present – all will rec-

ognize that there is no gain that you do not all participate in and no loss for which you do not all share the sacrifice.

As Avatars, you remember who you are and what you are not. You remember you are not things. You remember you are not any of the ideas of nationalism or race that humans fight over. You are neither expressions nor identities. You are the source of these things and you can create better.

Together you can work to feed the hungry, protect the environment and speak for peace – these are the efforts that buy you the time you need to expand Avatar and create an enlightened world. But ultimately, all these problems must be solved within the collective consciousness of humanity.

What you stand for is the balance into which all things will come. You must achieve that still point in your own lives and from that place share the experience of Avatar.

Not everyone will immediately appreciate your wisdom. When you run into someone who will not hear the lessons, you must look deeper within yourselves to find the idea that you project as wrong and the idea you embrace as right and resolve them. Then offer the lessons again. What you can't do from without, you can do from within. There is no longer the slightest doubt; you can anticipate and begin to celebrate the dawn of an enlightened civilization.

Your network of friends will grow forever. It is a joy to you and a shining example of sanity to future generations who will mark time by this period of world transformation.

Personally, I thank you for your time and the trust you have placed in me. I will forever remain faithful to the inexpressible union that we share now and will surely share again. It is our secret strength. We are together here and now, always. I love you.

Harry's Epilogue
Alignment

Since 1987 I have had the honor of meeting thousands of Avatar graduates. At first the meetings are a little awkward – they want to thank me for creating Avatar and I'm a little embarrassed by the praise. But the embarrassment is quickly replaced by a feeling of alignment and a deeply felt mutual respect. Two expressions of consciousness have managed to climb above the encumbering games of life and gaze at each other through moist eyes. There are no appropriate words nor any struggle to find any. There is no disciple. There is no master. Two companions, who experience a compassion for humanity that forms an inseparable bond.

I've seen the bond form between students from different countries and different backgrounds. I've witnessed a global network of companions awakening from a world that was drifting in an adversarial haze into a new world of understanding and cooperation. The new Avatars intuitively feel the excitement. There is a recognition of why the fates have gifted a certain talent or why life has favored the development of this or that skill. We're each an essential part of the same team!

Avatar created a worldwide mobilization of the spirit. What was once only a quiet, lonely hope struggling against the many beliefs in the eminent self-destruction of humankind, has become a rallying point. Something good has appeared.

If by reading this book, you sensed some intangible changes beginning to take place in your idea of what is possible, I am satisfied.

Boundless Love,

Harry Palmer

Alignment

If you feel an alignment
toward the goal of creating
an enlightened planetary
civilization and would like
to learn more about Avatar,
send your name and address to:

**Avatar Network Consultant
Star's Edge International
237 North Westmonte Drive
Altamonte Springs, Florida 32714
Phone (407) 788-3090
Fax (407) 788-1052**

Give The *Ultimate* Gift

Turn Your Friends On To
LIVING DELIBERATELY

Exclusive for people who already own a copy of Living Deliberately. Send us the name and address of a friend along with $17.00 ($15.00 plus S&H) and we'll send them a copy of Living Deliberately with a gift card in your name.

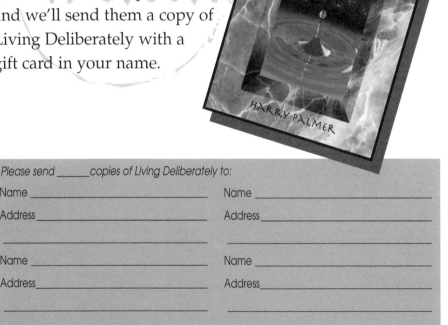

Please send _____ copies of Living Deliberately to:

Name _____   Name _____

Address _____   Address _____

_____   _____

Name _____   Name _____

Address _____   Address _____

_____   _____

From: _____

_____

Star's Edge International
237 North Westmonte Drive
Altamonte Springs, FL 32714

Bulk copies of Living Deliberately are available from Star's Edge at a substantial discount.
10 copies - $112.50, 25 copies - Inquire
50 copies - Inquire

For credit card orders, please call, (407) 788-3090 • Fax (407) 788-1052

Techniques For Exploring Consciousness By Harry Palmer

Experience a day of ReSurfacing
that will change the rest of your life!

ReSurfacing is a one day workshop that explores the relationship between belief and experience.

Name _____

Address _____

City, State, Zip Code _____

Phone_____

Avatar® and ReSurfacing® are registered trademarks of Star's Edge International

MORE INFORMATION

Section One of the Avatar® Marerials

Techniques For Exploring Consciousness By Harry Palmer

Experience a day of ReSurfacing
that will change the rest of your life!

ReSurfacing is a one day workshop that explores the relationship between belief and experience.

Name _____

Address _____

City, State, Zip Code _____

Phone_____

Avatar® and ReSurfacing® are registered trademarks of Star's Edge International

MORE INFORMATION

Place
Stamp
Here

Star's Edge International

Attn. Marketing Consultant
237 North Westmonte Drive
Altamonte Springs, FL 32714

Place
Stamp
Here

Star's Edge International

Attn. Marketing Consultant
237 North Westmonte Drive
Altamonte Springs, FL 32714